George Henry Calvert

Coleridge, Shelley, Goethe

George Henry Calvert

Coleridge, Shelley, Goethe

ISBN/EAN: 9783742852144

Manufactured in Europe, USA, Canada, Australia, Japa

Cover: Foto ©Thomas Meinert / pixelio.de

Manufactured and distributed by brebook publishing software
(www.brebook.com)

George Henry Calvert

Coleridge, Shelley, Goethe

COLERIDGE, SHELLEY, GOETHE.

COLERIDGE, SHELLEY, GOETHE.

BIOGRAPHIC ÆSTHETIC STUDIES.

BY

GEORGE H. CALVERT.

BOSTON:
LEE AND SHEPARD, PUBLISHERS.
NEW YORK:
CHARLES T. DILLINGHAM.

RIVERSIDE, CAMBRIDGE:
STEREOTYPED AND PRINTED BY
H. O. HOUGHTON AND COMPANY.

CONTENTS.

———————

COLERIDGE.

TO COLERIDGE.

COLERIDGE, for many a studious year I have been
Thy thankful mate; climbing the misty heights
Of speculation, or when — the delights
Of great imagination's realm serene
Blessing me through th' impassioned visions seen
By ravished genius — thou hast shown me sights,
Revealed to mighty Poets with the lights
Struck by creative frenzy; visions clean,
That mind in purgatorial surges dip,
And we come freshened forth, so purified,
That ever anew thy rich companionship
I court, to warm me at a holy fire,
And be with deep soul-logic stoutly plied,
Or trance-ensteeped by thy melodious lyre.

COLERIDGE.

I.

WHOEVER would write becomingly about Coleridge must admire him, and admire him with earnest thankfulness. Sympathy, — so essential to the biographer, aye, and to the full critic, — even a several-sided sympathy, were not enough. The warmth of admiration will enkindle to its tenderest our charity, and admiration and charity, with their united glow, will dissolve into vapor any thoughts on the weaknesses and failures of this remarkable man ; so that, if we think of them at all, we think of them only with a plaintive murmur, because through them we have been bereft of some of the harvest we had a right to expect from the healthful growth of such diverse and peerless powers. And even mildest murmur will be hushed, through sympathy with the sufferings his weaknesses caused to 'the author and man, our splendent gracious benefactor.

Were there left of Coleridge nothing but *Kubla Khan*, from this gem one might almost reconstruct, in full brightness, its great author's poetic work, just as the expert zoölogist reconstructs the extinct megatherium from a single fossil bone. Of this masterpiece, the chief beauty is not the noted music of the versification, but the range and quality of the imaginings embodied in this music. Were there in these no unearthly breathings, no mysterious grandeur, the verse could not have been made to pulsate so rhythmically. The essence of the melody is in the fineness of the conception, in the poetic imaginations. In this case, as in all cases, the spirit not only controls but creates the body. Metrical talent must be there to handle the molten words as they flow from the furnace of genius, shaping and placing them while still swollen with genial warmth. Genius, the master, cannot do without talent, the servant.

> " Five miles meandering with a mazy motion
> Through wood and dale the sacred river ran,
> Then reached the caverns measureless to man,
> And sank in tumult to a lifeless ocean : "

To present of a sudden to the mind a signal
thought, which springs unexpectedly but ap-
propriately out of another, the meeting of the
two striking a light that flashes a new and
brilliant ray upon the attention, — to do this
is to perform a high poetic feat. The sacred
river running through wood and dale, then
gliding into the earth through caverns measureless to man, to sink " in tumult to a lifeless
ocean : " this mysterious picture sets the mind
a brooding, awakens its poetic sensibility.
Suppose the passage had stopped here. Re-
galed by such a fresh, impressive presentation,
the mind would have grasped it as an inward
boon, to be held tightly hold of by the susceptible reader, awakening in him, through quick
affinities, thoughts of human fate and woe.
But the passage does not stop here ; in the
poet's mind, as in the capable reader's, are
generated associations with human destiny :
and so, instead of a full stop at "ocean," there
is only a colon, the poet's thought springing
forward into the two wonderful lines, —

> " And mid this tumult Kubla heard from far
> Ancestral voices prophesying war."

And the passage, instead of leaving on the
reader an impression of calm, strange beauty,

kindles into a startling splendor. The physical tumult passes into human tumult ; the
vague, hoarse swell of a torrent grows articu-
late, the "caverns measureless to man" deepen
into the abode of former kings, who, from the
subterranean darkness to which their warrior-
ambition has doomed them, throw upon the
ear of their Sardanapalean descendant doleful,
menacing predictions. All this, and more, is
in those two lines, so laden with meaning and
music, whereby the physical picture is magni-
fied, deepened, vivified, through psychical par-
ticipation. The poetical is ever an appeal to
the deepest in the human mind, and a great
burst of poetic light like this lays bare, for the
imagination to roam in, a vast indefinite domain.

In another part of the short poem is a similar sudden heightening of effect by the introduction of humanity into a scene of purely
terrene features :

> "But oh! that deep romantic chasm which slanted
> Down the green hill athwart a cedarn cover !
> A savage place! as holy and enchanted
> As e'er beneath a waning moon was haunted "

These lines could have been written only by a
poet with the finest ear, an internal ear. When

we come to the last word of the fourth line,
we pass into a higher region: "haunted!"
Haunted by what?

"By woman wailing for her demon lover."

On this single line is stamped the power of a
great poet; that is, a poet in whom breadth
and depth of intellectual and sympathetic endowment give to the refining aspiring poetic
faculty material to work upon drawn from the
grander, subtler, remoter resources of the human soul, — material beyond the reach of any
but poets of the first order, whose right, indeed, to a place in this order rests upon their
power of higher spiritual reach united to wider
intellectual range. How much is involved
in this short passage! A landscape gift, to
present in two lines a clear picture of the
"savage place;" then, by a leap of the poet's
imagination, the scene is overhung by an
earthly atmosphere that makes it so holy and
enchanted that (and here the poet takes the
final great leap) it is fit, "under a waning
moon," to be haunted

"By woman wailing for her demon lover."

That is a poetically imaginative leap of the
boldest and most beautiful. What an ethereal

springiness, what an intellectual swing, in the mind that could make such a leap! That particular one Coleridge's friend Wordsworth could not have made, strong as he was in poetic imagination. It implies almost something spectral, superearthly, something uncanny. And what an exquisitely musical rhythm the thought weaves about itself for its poetic incarnation.

Kubla Khan is a fragment, just as is a much longer, and his greatest, poem, *Christabel*. In the autumn of 1797 Coleridge, then in poor health, had retired to a lonely farmhouse on the confines of Somerset and Devonshire. One day, from the effect of an anodyne, prescribed to him, he fell asleep in his chair while reading in *Purchas's Pilgrimage* a passage like this: " Here the Khan Kubla commanded a palace to be built, and a stately garden thereunto ; and thus ten miles of fertile ground were enclosed with a wall." He slept about three hours. When he awoke he seemed to have composed two or three hundred lines describing what, in this sleep of the outward senses, he had inwardly seen and heard. So vivid was his recollection that immediately on awaking he seized a pen and began to write as one would when dictated to. In the midst of his writing he was called out on business. And he went out! Suppose a great statesman and orator, in the full swing of a grave momentous speech before a public assembly, to be suddenly interrupted and asked to listen to a young lady's dream! Not more impertinent were this than the interruption of Coleridge by a call of outward business. Nay, it were so much the less impertinent as the poetic dreams of Coleridge were more freighted with wisdom and enduring thought than any statesman's oration. To permit himself to be arrested in an immortal flight, as was this of *Kubla Khan!* to lay down his pen and go out to talk to some intruder, from a small neighboring town, about a prosaic, insignificant, transitory, delusive matter of fact! And he who was a bungler at these every-day opacities, and was an expert at translucent ideals. The business of Coleridge was to dream poetic dreams, not to act. So grand and new and beautiful and significant were his dreams that, like works of Art, they become stimulative and generative of high thoughts in others. In Coleridge there was so deep an inwardness that, when abstracted from the outer world,

2

whether in a trance-like sleep, as when he produced *Kubla Khan*, or in exalted soliloquy,
there poured forth, from large sources of sensibility and reason, streams of richly-worded
invention, floods of imaginative thought.

When, after a detention of an hour, he came
back and resumed his pen, the vision had
faded. And so, *Kubla Khan*, like other of
Coleridge's work, is a brilliant fragment.

Kubla Khan is likewise typical of Coleridge's poetry in that it is more spiritual than
passionate. Coleridge, while, as poet, appeal-
ing to and touching the feelings, was not a
man of fervent predominant desires. His
sensibilities — as sound as they were delicate
— were not fortified by depth and warmth
of passion : he was more tender than impassioned.

In its shining superexcellence the poetical
looks extravagant and visionary, in its prepo-
tency it seems preposterous. And this for the
same reason why, with our earthly eyes, we
cannot see any of the millions of spiritual
creatures that "walk the earth both when we
wake and when we sleep ;" our vision is not
enough spiritualized. The best function of the
poetical is to ascend to the interior spiritual

source ; and to follow it thither is not easy. The poetical is a divine flame, in whose transfiguring light the concrete grossness of earthly realities being fused, the causative law of their being becomes discernible. When in the Sermon on the Mount we are enjoined to "love your enemies, bless those that curse you, do good to them that hate you, and pray for them which despitefully use you and persecute you, that you may be the children of your Father which is in heaven," we listen in despair, all this so transcends our conceptions. These injunctions are a poetic ideal reached by the utterer of them through the sublime spirituality of his nature. Dwelling habitually on this upper plane, he was enabled to seize the higher possibilities of humanity. Like the Beatitudes and the rest of this transcendent Sermon, these injunctions are the poetry of the moral sense. To the sensuous, and still more to the sensual, ear they sound impracticable, Utopian. They are a voice from the supreme altitudes, proclaiming to what elevations we are capable of mounting.

In the *Ancient Mariner*, the hero of that great poem, after shooting the Albatross, exclaims,

> " And I had done a hellish thing,
> And it would work 'em woe :
> For all averred, I had killed the bird
> That made the breeze to blow.
> Ah, wretch ! said they, the bird to slay,
> That made the breeze to blow ! "

In thus reproaching him who had slain the Albatross, the crew obeyed a movement — by no means confined to superstitious sailors — of human shortsightedness, whereby men would fain force the moral law to square with their temporary desires. When the crew perceived that the breeze did not cease, and that the fog had disappeared,

> " Then all averred, I had killed the bird
> That brought the fog and mist.
> 'T was right, said they, such birds to slay,
> That bring the fog and mist.
> The fair breeze blew, the white foam flew,
> The furrow followed free ;
> We were the first that ever burst
> Into that silent sea."

Thus they sped until they reached the Line. Then the breeze suddenly ceased to blow. In a copper sky the Sun at noon stood right above the perpendicular mast. In the air was no breath ; the vessel, without motion, as if pinned to the spot, was

> " As idle as a painted ship
> Upon a painted ocean."

And now the water gave out :

> " Water, water, everywhere,
> Nor any drop to drink."

Their lips were baked, their tongues withered at the root. Upon the Anoient Mariner evil looks were turned :

> " Ah ! well-a-day ! what evil looks
> Had I from old and young !
> Instead of the cross, the Albatross
> About my neck was hung."

A sail ! a sail ! Hope flattered their sinking souls. But strange ! as the ship descried passes between them and the setting sun the face of the sun is crossed as with bars. The sail was but the skeleton-phantom of a ship. She came along side ! On the deck are two figures, Death and a woman (a harlot, symbol of death in life), playing at dice :

> " The game is done ! I 've won ! I 've won !
> Quoth she, and whistles thrice."

She had won the Ancient Mariner, but the crew is doomed.

To give life to these fantastical imaginations is needed a poet's and a thinker's thought, and

to give to the poet's thought depth and significance is needed spirituality, with a strong sense
of moral sovereignty. What is more flat and
unprofitable than to hear a prosaic man tell his
dreams? That tales to which vivacity is imparted by poetic imaginativeness are nevertheless shallow and unattractive when wanting a
moral background, is learnt when one attempts
to reread the prose tales of Poe. Behind their
fantasy are no depths; their ingenuity is bar-
ren; there is no issue out of their horrors.
They lack what, notwithstanding their spectral quality, Hawthorne's tales have, humanity.
The *Ancient Mariner* is steeped in humanity. And then, to these visionary inventions a
charm is imparted by their inward truth. For,
besides that the visions have their birth in feeling, in a gifted being like Coleridge his supernatural would be true to nature, because having in himself, like every other human creature,
both the supernatural and the natural, — being
bound alike to heaven and to earth, — his perceptions and his imaginations are illuminated
by the revealing light both of reason and of
genius.

This light it is which, casting such exquisite
shadows, makes the *Ancient Mariner* to sparkle

with irresistible fascination. The fearful penalty which follows an act so thoughtless, seemingly indifferent, comparatively innocent, as that of shooting an albatross, might be called the poetry of retribution. It is an ascension to the superior spiritual source, an ascension which the poet, through the elevation of his nature, is empowered to achieve, and which his æsthetic gifts enabled him to present in a captivating garb. The story of the Ancient Mariner and the crew implicated in his act is a voice from the supreme heights, which, uttered through a gifted poet, comes accompanied by weird, musical, significant extravagances.

Among the high qualities of the *Ancient Mariner* the highest is the symbolical meaning discernible on the brightest pages, peering through a supersensual radiance, giving intenseness to sparkles of poetry. Everywhere the intellectual vivacity is unflagging, and the whole is quickened by a profound moral which, though not obtruded, is uttered by the old sailor, who ends his strange tale with these deep, tuneful words :

> " Farewell ! farewell ! but this I tell
> To thee, thou Wedding guest !

He prayeth well, who loveth well
Both man and bird and beast.

" He prayeth best, who loveth best
All things both great and small ;
For the dear God who loveth us,
He made and loveth all."

The same sound, beautiful moral shines
through as through Wordsworth's *Hart-leap
Well :*

" One lesson, Shepherd, let us two divide,
Taught by what Nature shows, and what conceals ;
Never to blend our pleasure or our pride
With sorrow of the meanest thing that feels."

Coleridge was one of the most original of
men ; that is, in his mind there was a light so
individual and strong that on human conditions and relations it cast fresh illumination ;
and thence, since he wrote and talked, the
problems of life are less enigmatical, its spiritual capabilities more apparent, its hopes more
assured and more elevated. Like some other
men of his high order Coleridge was too original to be at once appreciated. To men of routine there is offensiveness in originality. Some
people have an honest difficulty in appreciating
and appropriating fresh thought. Some, when
they have the culture and insight to discern

new power, have not the frankness to speak out; and the taking of a pen in one's hand, far from always bracing one's moral responsibility, often relaxes it, through the temptation offered by the pen to blacken a rival, or to lame a fresh competitor who looks formidable.

From honest ignorance and dishonest detraction Coleridge, like his friend Wordsworth, had, from the very originality of his genius and the superiority of his gifts, to suffer more than most new candidates for literary honors. In the short preface to *Christabel* he thus, in his gentle way, refers to one of the charges brought against him by some of that class of writers called critics, but who often deserve not the high name ; for, etymologically, critic implies competency to judge. Coleridge says : " There is amongst us a set of critics who seem to hold that every possible thought or image is traditional ; who have no notion that there are such things as fountains in the world, small as well as great; and would therefore charitably derive every rill they see flowing from a perforation made in some other man's tank."

Against the *Ancient Mariner* and *Christabel*

hostile criticism was as powerless as a snow-storm would be to quench Hecla in full eruption, or earth-fogs permanently to obscure the stars.

As in the *Ancient Mariner*, so in *Christabel*, excellence is aimed at by "interesting the affections through the dramatic truth of such emotions as would naturally accompany such situations, supposing them·real." In both the chief originality consists, not in the supernatural frame in which the tales are set, — an invention supplied by mere fancy, — but in the quality of the poetic imagination displayed in the management of the story and in particular conjunctions. Were the whole six hundred lines of *Christabel* (for unhappily there are no more) in their general quality unelastic, unimaginative, instead of being, as they are, buoyant and sparkling, every page vivid with intellectual activity, musical with poetic feeling, still one would be repaid for the reading of every paragraph, in order not to miss just these two lines which conclude the exquisite description of the Lady Christabel praying by moonlight under the old oak tree :

> " And both blue eyes more bright than clear,
> Each about to have a tear."

Coleridge had his share of earthly affliction, — more than his share, we might say, had not much of his distress been of his own making. But whatever his burthens, they were counter-weighed by the joy of harboring within himself, and projecting upon others, such thoughts. How blessed the brain in whose inlets nestled a perfumed gem like this :

> " Quoth Christabel, — so let it be :
> And as the lady bade did she.
> Her gentle limbs did she undress,
> And lay down in her loveliness."

All three of these poems, *Christabel*, the *Ancient Mariner*, and *Kubla Khan*, were written when Coleridge was in his twenty-fifth or twenty-sixth year. In each of them are beauties which so move our admiration they give us thrills which deeply touch and teach the soul. What was the individuality whence issued such superlative products ? As easily can lightning be tracked to its lair as genius : both have their birth in a fiery creative centre, too vivid with heat and light to be penetrated or approached. But the conditions under which they flash into exhibition can be studied, and of the medium through which the revelation is made something may be learnt.

II

THE father of Coleridge was simple-minded, learned, eccentric. At the age of sixteen he quitted the house of his impoverished parents, receiving a blessing and the half of his father's last crown. He had walked but a few miles when, overcome by thoughts of his destitution, he sat down by the roadside and wept aloud. A gentleman happening to pass by recognized the son of his neighbor, took him home, and sent him to school. Here he was a hard student, married at nineteen, shortly after his marriage entered Sidney College, Cambridge, distinguished himself there in Hebrew and mathematics, and, had he not been married, would have been rewarded with a fellowship. On leaving college he became a teacher in Southampton, was afterwards appointed headmaster of the school at Ottery St. Mary, Devonshire, and obtained the living of the parish. His son, the poet, thus speaks of him : " My father was a good mathematician, and well versed in the Greek, Latin, and Hebrew lan-

guages. He published, or rather attempted to
publish, several works. He made the world
his confidant with respect to his learning and
ingenuity, and the world seems to have kept
the secret very faithfully. His various works,
unthumbed, uncut, were preserved free from
all pollution in the family archives. This piece
of good luck promises to be hereditary ; for all
my compositions have the same amiable home-
staying propensity. The truth is, my father
was not a first-rate genius ; he was, however,
a first-rate Christian, which is much better. In
learning, goodheartedness, absentness of mind,
and excessive ignorance of the world, he was
a perfect Parson Adams."

The poet's mother, Anna Bowdon, was the
second wife of the vicar. Of their ten children, nine sons and one daughter, Samuel Taylor, born October 21, 1772, was the youngest.
The mother was an admirable economist and
manager. She managed so well that she got
her sons started in professional careers, in the
army, the church, the navy. The unambitious
vicar was willing that they should be brought
up to trades, except the youngest, Samuel
Taylor, the child of his latter years, who, he
resolved, should be a parson. Several of the

poet's brothers died young, and his only sister, Anne, at twenty-one. Her he has immortalized in two lines :

"Rest, gentle Shade, and wait thy Maker's will ; Then rise unchanged, and be an angel still !"

Circumstances, literally what stands around a man, being the offspring of general human activity, react upon individual human beings with irresistible effect. Men and circumstances, being of one blood, are indissolubly interwoven for weal or woe. Men make circumstances, and circumstances mold men. Even the most original natures, natures of such deep prolific power of soul that their mission is to generate new circumstances, whereby to lift human life to higher levels, even they cannot escape the pressure of present conditions.

One of these generative minds was Samuel Taylor Coleridge, a mind of such inward vitality that it poured fresh streams into the accumulated reservoirs of human thought. The mental movement which at its noon has the exceptional liveliness and momentum to generate new circumstances is apt in its morning to break from routine into a path of its own making.

That in his early surroundings Coleridge
was not so favored as his friend Wordsworth
is apparent from the subjoined account by
himself of his childhood from his fourth to his
ninth year. Wordsworth, to be sure, with his
decision and will, would have so reacted upon
such surroundings as to have modified or even
changed them. For, of those who have in
them the inborn force to make new circumstances it is the privilege (when they have the
will and the self-control of a Wordsworth) to
resist and in some measure to baffle existing ones. Coleridge was more passive, more
practically helpless than his illustrious friend.
This passage, so valuable as biography, is
worth something as premonition. But parents
and teachers are irremediably incapable of
discerning in the wayward sensitive boy an
exceptional poetic genius, who ought to have
exceptional treatment. Seldom does autobiog-
raphy furnish a page so lively and instructive.

" From October, 1775, to October, 1778.
These three years I continued at the reading
school, because I was too little to be trusted
among my father's school-boys. . . . . My father was very fond of me, and I was my
mother's darling ; in consequence whereof I

was very miserable. For Molly, who had nursed my brother Francis [next above Samuel Taylor in age], and was immoderately fond of him, hated me because my mother took more notice of me than of Frank ; and Frank hated me because my mother gave me now and then a bit of cake when he had none, — quite forgetting that for one bit of cake which I had and he had not, he had twenty sops in the pan, and pieces of bread and butter with sugar on them, from Molly, from whom I received only thumps and ill names.

"So I became fretful, and timorous, and a tell-tale ; and the school-boys drove me from play, and were always tormenting me. And hence I took no pleasure in boyish sports, but read incessantly. I read through all gilt-cover little books that could be had at that time, and likewise all the uncovered tales of *Tom Hick-athrift, Jack the Giant-Killer*, and the like. And I used to lie by the wall, and mope ; and my spirits used to come upon me suddenly, and in a flood; and then I was accustomed to run up and down the churchyard, and act over again all I had been reading on the docks, the nettles, and the rank grass. At six years of age I remember to have read *Belisarius, Rob-*

inson Crusoe, and *Philip Quarles;* and then I found the *Arabian Nights' Entertainments*, one tale of which (the tale of a man who was compelled to seek for a pure virgin) made so deep an impression on me (I had read it in the evening while my mother was at her needle) that I was haunted by spectres whenever I was in the dark : and I distinctly recollect the anxious and fearful eagerness with which I used to watch the window where the book lay, and when the sun came upon it I would seize it, carry it by the wall, and bask and read. My father found out the effect which these books had produced, and burned them.

"So I became a dreamer, and acquired an indisposition to all bodily activity ; and I was fretful, and inordinately passionate ; and as I could not play at anything, and was slothful, I was despised and hated by the boys : and because I could read and spell, and had, I may truly say, a memory and understanding forced into almost unnatural ripeness, I was flattered and wondered at by all the old women. And so I became very vain, and despised most of the boys that were at all near my own age, and before I was eight years old I was a *character.* Sensibility, imagination, vanity, sloth,

3

and feelings of deep and bitter contempt for almost all who traversed the orbit of my understanding, were even then prominent and manifest.

"From October, 1778, to 1779. That which I began to be from three to six, I continued to be from six to nine. In this year I was admitted into the Grammar School, and soon outstripped all of my age."

Here is another relation of similar interest. Very rare are such autobiographic notes on the childhood of poets. How near were *Christabel* and the *Ancient Mariner* being sacrificed to that tender sensitiveness, that delicacy of cerebral fibre, out of which they grew!

"I had asked my mother one evening to cut my cheese entire, so that I might toast it. This was no easy matter, it being a *crumbly* cheese. My mother however did it. I went into the garden for something or other, and in the mean time my brother Frank minced my cheese, to 'disappoint the favorite.' I returned, saw the exploit, and in an agony of passion flew at Frank. He pretended to have been seriously hurt by my blow, flung himself on the ground, and there lay with outstretched limbs. I hung over him mourning and in a

great fright; he leaped up, and with a horse-
laugh gave me a severe blow in the face. I
seized a knife, and was running at him, when
my mother came in and took me by the arm.
I expected a flogging, and, struggling from
her, I ran away to a little hill or slope, at the
bottom of which the Otter flows, about a mile
from Ottery. There I stayed, my rage died
away, but my obstinacy vanquished my fears,
and taking out a shilling book, which had at
the end morning and evening prayers, I very
devoutly repeated them — thinking at the
same time with a gloomy inward satisfaction
— how miserable my mother must be! I distinctly remember my feelings, when I saw a
Mr. Vaughan pass over the bridge at about
a furlong's distance, and how I watched the
calves in the fields beyond the river. It grew
dark, and I fell asleep. It was towards the
end of October, and it proved a stormy night.
I felt the cold in my sleep, and dreamed that
I was pulling the blanket over me, and actually
pulled over me a dry thorn-bush which lay on
the ground near me. In my sleep I had rolled.
from the top of the hill till within three yards
of the river, which flowed by the unfenced
edge of the bottom. I awoke several times,

and finding myself wet, and cold, and stiff, closed my eyes again that I might forget it.

"In the mean time my mother waited about half an hour, expecting my return when the *sulks* had evaporated. I not returning, she sent into the churchyard, and round the town. Not found! Several men and all the boys were sent out to ramble about and seek me. In vain! My mother was almost distracted; and at ten o'clock at night I was *cried* by the crier in Ottery, and in two villages near it, with a reward offered for me. No one went to bed; indeed, I believe half the town were up all the night. To return to myself. About five in the morning, or a little after, I was broad awake, and attempted to get up and walk; but I could not move. I saw the shepherds and workmen at a distance, and cried, but so faintly, that it was impossible to hear me thirty yards off. And there I might have lain and died; for I was now almost given over, the ponds and even the river, near which I was lying, having been dragged. But providentially Sir Stafford Northcote, who had been out all night, resolved to make one other trial, and came so near that he heard me crying. He carried me in his arms for nearly a

quarter of a mile, when we met my father and
Sir Stafford Northcote's servants. I remember, and never shall forget, my father's face as
he looked upon me while I lay in the servant's
arms — so calm, and the tears stealing down
his face ; for I was the child of his old age.
My mother, as you may suppose, was outrage-
ous with joy. Meantime in rushed a young
lady, crying out, 'I hope you'll whip him,
Mrs. Coleridge.' This woman still lives at
Ottery ; and neither philosophy nor religion
has been able to conquer the antipathy which
I feel towards her, whenever I see her. I was
put to bed, and recovered in a day or so. But
I was certainly injured ; for I was weakly and
subject to ague for many years after."

One can see the worthy, tender-souled vicar,
tears of joy stealing down his face. A terrible blow to him would have been the death of
his dear little boy in that way, and a calamity
to all whose language is English would have
been the cutting short of a life so laden with
literary genius. I beg to add to that of Coleridge my detestation — a by no means un-
philosophical or irreligious feeling — of the
"young lady" with the ready whip. This was
a hundred years ago in custom-ridden Eng-

land. To our shame in America the rod is still legal in some of our public schools. Colts and cubs are trained and taught more efficiently through love than through fear. What then must be the diabolism of the rod applied to the young immortals of human kind?

This excellent man, John Coleridge, vicar of Ottery St. Mary, and head-master of the King's school, died when his son, Samuel Taylor, was in his ninth year. Connected with his death are two incidents, curious enough to be retold. On his return from Plymouth (whither he had been to start his son Francis for India as midshipman under Admiral Graves), arriving late in the afternoon at Exeter, some friends kindly pressed him to stay all night. He declined because, although, as he said, not superstitious, he had a dream the night before that Death had appeared to him and touched him with his dart. When he reached home the family were up to receive him, all except the youngest, Samuel Taylor, who was asleep in bed. The vicar was in fine spirits and apparently in good health, and told his wife his dream of the night before. On going to bed he complained of a pain in the bowels, to which he was subject. She gave

him some peppermint; he lay down again, saying he was better. In a few moments his wife
heard a noise in his throat, and spoke to him;
but he made no answer. Again she spoke,
and again, without answer. Her shriek awoke
little Samuel, who cried out, "Papa is dead!"

Thirty years afterwards Coleridge, referring
to the death of his father, exclaimed: "Oh!
that I might so pass away, if, like him, I were
an Israelite without guile! The image of my
father, my revered, kind, learned, simple-hearted
father, is a religion to me."

The death of his father made an important
change in the schooling of Coleridge. Judge
Buller, a friend and former pupil of the vicar,
obtained for his son, Samuel Taylor, admission
into Christ's Hospital, the celebrated blue-coat
free school of London. Coleridge was about
ten years of age when he went to London.
Before entering Christ's Hospital he spent
two months with his uncle, Mr. Bowdon. This
visit is thus described by himself: "Mr. Bowdon was generous as the air, and a man of
very considerable talents, but he was fond, as
others have been, of his bottle. He received
me with great affection, and I stayed ten weeks
at his house, during which I went occasionally

to Judge Buller's.   My uncle was very proud
of me, and used to carry me from 'coffee-house
to coffee-house, and tavern to tavern, where I
drank, and talked, and disputed, as if I had
been a man.   Nothing was more common than
for a large party to exclaim in my hearing, that
I was a prodigy, and so forth ; so that while I
remained at my uncle's I was most completely
spoilt and pampered, both mind and body."

Within the walls of Christ's Hospital were
then lodged seven hundred boys, one third of
them, like Coleridge, the sons of clergymen.
For boys, hardly less than for girls, a daily,
hourly need is woman's care and affection.
Of human life love is the very sun, that warms
and swells it into bloom.   For the opening
feelings and faculties of childhood love does
what solar rays do for the sprouting plant,
that would wither and die without their down-
streaming parental glow.   By removal from
the maternal fireside Coleridge was not entirely cut off from womanly tenderness.   The
numerous school was divided into twelve dor-
mitories with a matron for each.   Then there
was, in those days, the head-master's wife, a
woman with a heart large enough to be a
motherly friend of all the boys.   A grateful

memory of her Coleridge carried into his latest years; only a short time before his death he thus spoke of her: "No tongue can express good Mrs. Bowyer. Val le Grice and I were once going to be flogged for some domestic misdeed, and Bowyer was thundering away at us by way of prologue when Mrs. B. looked in and said, 'Flog them soundly, sir, I beg!' This saved us. Bowyer was so nettled at the interruption that he growled out, 'Away, woman, away!' and we were let off." Here is also a reminiscence, from the same page of the *Table Talk*, of Bowyer himself. "The discipline at Christ's Hospital in my time was ultra-Spartan; all domestic ties were to be put aside. 'Boy!' I remember Bowyer saying to me once when I was crying the first day of my return after the holidays, 'Boy! the school is your father; Boy! the school is your mother; Boy! the school is your brother; Boy! the school is your sister; the school is your first cousin, and your second cousin, and all the rest of your relations! Let's have no more crying!'"

Nevertheless, Bowyer may be looked upon as one of the good fortunes of Coleridge's life. An admirable instructor, he was, what

is very rare in a professional pedagogue, a
sound, penetrating critic, — a superiority of
slight avail to the common run of boy-learners,
but of profound service to one of uncommon
literary capacity. Coleridge, among whose
virtues was a cordial gratefulness, thus speaks
of Bowyer in the *Biographia Literaria:*

" At school (Christ's Hospital) I enjoyed
the inestimable advantage of a very sensible,
though at the same time a very severe, master, the Reverend James Bowyer. He early
molded my taste to the preference of Demos-
thenes to Cicero, of Homer and Theocritus
to Virgil, and again of Virgil to Ovid. He
habituated me to compare Lucretius (in such
extracts as I then read), Terence, and above
all the chaster poems of Catullus, not only
with the Roman poets of the so-called silver
and brazen ages, but with even those of the
Augustan era : and on the ground of plain
sense and universal logic to see and assert
the superiority of the former in the truth and
nativeness both of their thoughts and diction.
At the same time that we were studying the
Greek tragic poets, he made us read Shakespeare and Milton as lessons : and they were
the lessons, too, which required most time and

trouble to *bring up*, so as to escape his cen-
sure. I learned from him that poetry, even
that of the loftiest and, seemingly, that of the
wildest odes, had a logic of its own, as severe
as that of science ; and more difficult, because
more subtle, more complex, and dependent on
more and more fugitive causes. ·In the truly
great poets, he would say, there is a reason
assignable, not only for every word, but for the
position of every word ; and I well remember
that, availing himself of the synonyms to the
Homer of Didymus, he made us attempt to
show, with regard to each, why it would not
have answered the same purpose, and wherein
consisted the peculiar fitness of the word in
the original text.

"In our own English composition (at least
for the last three years of our school education), he showed no mercy to phrase, metaphor,
or image, unsupported by a sound sense, or
where the same sense might have been conveyed with equal force and dignity in plainer
words. *Lute, harp*, and *lyre, Muse, Muses*, and
inspirations, Pegasus, Parnassus, and *Hippo-
crene*, were all an abomination to him."

In his boyhood Coleridge was a gluttonous
devourer of books, for thus may be translated

the phrase he applies to himself, *helluo libro-*
rum. It was a diseased, omnivorous appetite.
A characteristic incident opened the way for
its boundless indulgence. Walking one day
in the Strand with eyes half closed, the better
to give play to his inward senses, he imagined
himself Leander swimming the Hellespont,
and making the motions to correspond, one of
his little hands came in contact with the coat
pocket of a gentleman, who, turning quickly,
charged him with a design of pocket-picking,
but, looking into his ingenuous face, accepted
at once his denial, and, engaging him in talk,
was so struck with his knowledge and intelligence that he made him free of a circulating
library in King Street, Cheapside. Here he
was entitled to two volumes a day, and would
steal out to get them. Then, crumpling himself up into a sunny corner, he would read,
read, read! "Conceive," he says, "what I
must have been at fourteen." At fifteen "I
had bewildered myself in metaphysics and in
theologic controversy." So immersed and fascinated was he that nothing else pleased him.
History and particular facts lost all interest
to his mind. Poetry, and even novels and romances, became insipid. In his wanderings

on *leave-days*, his greatest delight was to get into conversation with any passer, especially if he were dressed in black, for he soon directed the talk to his favorite subjects,

> " Of providence, foreknowledge, will, and fate,
> Fixed fate, free will, foreknowledge absolute,
> And found no end, in wandering mazes lost."

In after years Coleridge deplored the effects of getting absorbed into these abstruse arguments, which, he says, "exercise the strength and subtlety of the understanding without awakening the feelings of the heart." From this unwholesome pursuit he was withdrawn, partly by the accidental introduction to an amiable family, but chiefly by the poetry of Bowles, the tenderness and naturalness of which were well fitted to attract and influence at that time a precocious, genial boy.

From want of direction what waste of a great mind's resources in its early overflow! In the budding season genius needs sympathetic guidance, tender supervision ; but where, in our actual organization, is to be had the insight and the sympathy? These are at present little available for this fine function. As schools go, a Coleridge was in rare luck to have fallen into the hands of a genuine critic like Bowyer. To have founded at Christ's Hospital such a friendship as that with Charles Lamb was another piece of good fortune. In his reminiscences of these school-days Lamb exclaims : —

"Come back into memory, like as thou wast in the day-spring of thy fancies, with hope like a fiery column before thee, — the dark pillar not yet turned — Samuel Taylor Coleridge, Logician, Metaphysician, Bard! How have I seen the casual passer through the cloister stand still, intranced with admiration (while he weighed the disproportion between the *speech* and the *garb* of the young Mirandola) to hear thee unfold, in thy deep and sweet intonations, the mysteries of Iamblichus, or Plotinus (for even in those years thou waxed not pale at such philosophic draughts), or reciting Homer in his Greek, or Pindar, — while the walls of the old Grey Friars reëchoed to the accents of the *inspired charity boy!*"

By his scholarship and acquirement at Christ's Hospital, during his long abode there of eight years, Coleridge earned an appointment, by the head-master, to Cambridge. He was eighteen years of age when he entered

Jesus College.   In the summer of 1791, only
a few months after his entrance, he gained the
gold medal for the Greek Ode.   But at Cambridge, as at Christ's Hospital, he was a voracious reader of miscellaneous books rather
than a close.student of the college course.
Mathematics were neglected.   He took little
exercise.   His delight was to talk, and this,
from his school-days to the last year of his life,
was his chief daily enjoyment.

Taking into account the range of his knowledge and of his sympathies, his flow of fittest
words and sure memory, the poetic light aglow
within him, which gave a captivating luminousness to all the currents of his affluent mind,
together with the innate logical exaction that
kept these currents within their proper banks,
and recalling the joyful facility he always had
in the oral pouring forth of his rich accumula-
tions, and not less rich postulations, it may be
believed that Coleridge was the most eloquent
and eminent and instructive talker told of in
literature.

This gift was a magnet that at Cambridge
drew such of his fellow-students as had enough
in them to enjoy good talk, and made the room
of Coleridge ("the ground-floor room· on the

right hand of the staircase facing the great gate ") a constant rendezvous, says one of the frequenters. Those were angry times. By the heat of the French Revolution, then at boiling point, were fast engendered passionate pamphlets. Ever and anon came one from Burke. There was no need, says this reporter, to have the book present : Coleridge had read it in the morning, and could repeat whole pages in the evening *verbatim.*

The talk and studies had a strange interruption. In the autumn of 1793, from despondency on account of some debts, aggravated, it is believed, by a love-affair, Coleridge suddenly left Cambridge for London. The few shillings in his pocket were soon spent, and, attracted by a recruiting-advertisement, he enlisted as a private in the Fifteenth Regiment of Light Dragoons.

This extraordinary step — a leap in the dark downwards — should not be hastily imputed to the eccentricity of genius. Genius, as the originator, the initiator, in human affairs, is eccentric, flashing into new paths, into fresh domains, hereby giving proof of its superiority through its eccentricity. To be sure, it is liable to minor exhibitions, which are neither tokens of its worth nor useful to mankind. But this sudden move on the part of Coleridge was due to a kind of lawlessness caused by want of strength to tighten the cords that control that helm of man's life, a practical, resolute will. It came from the man, not from the poet. This kind of eccentricity Wordsworth never would have given in to, nor Shelley, nor Byron, nor Keats, nor Milton, nor Shakespeare. Of a more passive nature than any of these, his great compeers, was Coleridge, with less faculty of self-direction. Poets are, of course, and according to the degree of their creative force, more liable than other men to impulsions from within ; but such projection is on planes of thought, not on planes of action, and in Coleridge this poetic sensibility was not accompanied by a strong enough sense of the import of outward movements in the daily prosaic world of roofs and meals under them.

When asked his name by the enlisting officer, Coleridge answered, *Cumberback*, a name, he says, his horse would have deemed most suitable, so little equestrian were his habits. To preserve his proper initials, to this he prefixed *Silas Titus.* For bad riding and

worse grooming he made amends in the troop
by nursing the sick and writing letters for the
well. He was a dragoon for four months.
One day an officer found freshly written with
pencil on the stable door : " *Eheu! quam in-
fortunii miserrimum est fuisse felicem !* " The
writer was discovered to be *Cumberback*, whose
condition the words suited so well. But the
termination of his military career was brought
about through his being recognized by an acquaintance on the street in Reading, where the
regiment was stationed. Information being
given to his family, he was, after some difficulty, discharged on the 10th of April, 1794.

III.

An eventful year was 1794 to Coleridge. He went back to the University, and in the summer-vacation started with a companion for a tour in Wales, stopping on the way in Oxford to see a friend. Here he met Robert Southey. The two genial young men took to each other warmly. The minds of both were buoyant with literary projects, alight with sunny hopes. Both were hungry for knowledge, eager to sharpen their minds on other minds ; both were aglow with refined aspirations. Only a keen-sighted observer could then, in their effervescent young manhood, have perceived how radically diverse were the mental structures of these two. The one was to be a versatile, contemporaneous, literary purveyor, the other was destined to rank among the world's profoundest thinkers, a man whose thinking will be precious to future ages ; the one a voluminous, clever versifier, the other a richly-gifted, exquisite poet. The comparatively shallow mind of the one could

.

impart little to the deep creative resources of
the other. Nevertheless, through his prudent,
methodical, industrious living, and through his
generosity and affectionateness, the versatile
litterateur Southey was enabled in after years
to give shelter for some time to the family of
the profound, original, thriftless Coleridge.

Not the literary fruit it bore gave significance to the meeting with Southey, but its
practical consequences to the life of Coleridge ;
for it designated the ticket he took in the lot-
tery of marriage. After his excursion into
Wales he went to Bristol by appointment with
Southey, who here introduced him to Lovell, a
young Quaker, just married to Mary Fricker,
through whom Coleridge got acquainted with
Sarah, her elder sister, who shortly after became his wife, Southey marrying a third sister, Edith.

Under the aspiring impulse which has, at
different periods, moved other young men to
make an effort to emerge out of the injustices
and artificialities and multiform egoisms of
the actual, very imperfect, social organization, and create around them a healthier, less
smothery, self-loaded atmosphere, these three
friends formed a plan to found in America, on

the banks of the Susquehanna, a community one of whose predominant principles should be the abolition of individual property. The project came to nothing : it was another protest against existing social relations, another sigh for emancipation from obstructive, debasing slaveries, the chains of which, being self-imposed, will some day be shattered. The possibilities of man, even in his earthly sphere, are almost infinite. From the customs, ways, conditions of Timbuctoo who could infer the conditions and institutions, political, legal, moral, social, æsthetical, of London or Paris or New York ? Out of human upreachings and mental capabilities will be evolved social and industrial conditions to which those that the most advanced of Christendom now enjoy will seem as crude and insufficient as do to us those of Timbuctoo. And this will be achieved by cultivated aspiring thought, working under the sway of a sympathetic discoverer.

In the beginning of September Coleridge quitted Bath, where Southey then was, and where the Fricker family lived, and went back for the last time to Cambridge. Here he published *The Fall of Robespierre*, in part written by Southey, a tragedy whose chief interest is

that it was the first poem published by Coleridge, whose genius was hardly more dramatic
than that of his friend Wordsworth. Moreover, the play was written in the very year of
the overwhelming event it commemorates, an
event so deeply active as to shake a poet's faculties out of the moral calm which is a cardinal
condition for poetic creativeness. Moreover,
Coleridge's part, a third of the whole and about
three hundred lines, was written in two days.

On leaving the University, where he took
no degree, Coleridge entered manhood vigor-
ously and resolutely, devoting the spring and
summer of 1795 to giving lectures in Bristol.
The first six presented a comparative view of
the Civil War under Charles I. and the French
Revolution, their spirit vehemently hostile to
the policy of Pitt, but at the same time anti-
Jacobinical. Another course of six lectures
followed on "Revealed Religion, its Corruptions and its Political Views," written in the
Unitarian spirit. In his school-boy days of
omnivorous reading Coleridge had coquetted
with skepticism, which the stout Bowyer looked
upon as a breach of the rules, demanding, not
an appeal to the brain with argument, but an
application of birch to a less noble part. In

his early manhood Coleridge preached occasionally in a Unitarian chapel in Taunton, and
with such eloquence as to draw crowded audiences. His Unitarianism lasted but a few
years, and his relapse into Orthodoxy cost him
the good will of Unitarians, they never recov-
ering from the disappointment of having failed
to secure, after hooking, this lively leviathan.
Their spite they show by a studied deprecia-
tion.of Coleridge, which in people of so much
culture cannot be wholly sincere, — a depre-
ciation which is costly, inasmuch as it closes
or dims to them the pages of one of the richest writers and largest thinkers of all the ages.

On the 4th of October, 1795, Coleridge was
married to Sarah Fricker. They went to reside for a time at Clevedon on the Bristol
Channel.

This was not a well assorted union. Coleridge, with inordinate development of the reasoning, emotional, and poetic mental elements,
with deficiency of the determinative and the
self-seeking impulses, needed in his life-partner
the supplementary gifts of energy and will, to
make out of two halves a prosperous conjugal
whole. These gifts Mrs. Coleridge does not
seem to have possessed in force enough to

counteract the practical inertness of her husband, to inspirit him under failures and discouragement. With a mind so far ranging, original, poetical, as was that of Coleridge, full sympathy was not to be looked for, nor was it necessary on the part of his wife ; but Mrs. Coleridge seems to have had none. In this respect his friend Wordsworth was far more favored, not to speak of his noble sister, who was a second life-partner, and an especial mental helpmate. Nor was Wordsworth deficient where Coleridge was : he had a shrewd business talent. When, some years after Jeffrey's impotent attempt to crush Wordsworth as a poet, they first met, at a dinner-party in London, Jeffrey said that had he not been told who it was, he should have taken Wordsworth for a knowing man of the world.

Three days after his marriage Coleridge, his mind brimming with happiness and hope, wrote from Clevedon to a friend, that from their cottage he had a variegated land and sea view. Those were Coleridge's few halcyon days. His lovely bride was within the cottage ; his young, earnest brain teemed with confident purposes. His plan then was to return to Cambridge, finish " my great work on

Imitationes," and then issue a prospectus for a
school. There was some project of a monthly
magazine. But that, he says in the letter, he
gives up as "a thing of monthly anxiety and
quotidian bustle." This was written on the
7th of October, 1795. And yet, in Decem-
ber, only a few weeks later, he set zealous-
ly about to establish a weekly journal to be
called *The Watchman.* The design in estab-
lishing *The Watchman* was set forth in its
motto : *that all might know the truth and that
the truth might make us free.* Not only so, but
with a pocket full of flaming prospectuses,
Coleridge sallied forth in his own person to
get subscribers. In these years of his early
manhood Coleridge was a Liberal (not a Rad-
ical) in politics and a Unitarian in religion.

The canvassing for the paper (think of the
author of *Christabel* thus engaged !) he entered upon in Birmingham, and his first appeal
was to a rigid Calvinist, a tallow-chandler, a
tall, dingy man, with lank, dark, hard countenance. But he was a true lover of liberty, and
had proved to the satisfaction of many that
Mr. Pitt was one of the horns of the second
Beast in *The Revelation*, that spake as a drag-
on. After uttering some imperfect sentences

his introducer, a citizen of Birmingham, gave
the cause into the hands of his principal. Determined that no pains should be spared on his
part, and that he would present his case ex-
haustively, Coleridge commenced an harangue
of half an hour, varying his notes through the
whole gamut of eloquence "from the ratioci-
native to the declamatory, and in the latter
from the pathetic to the indignant. I argued,
I described, I promised, I prophesied; and beginning with the captivity of nations I ended
with the near approach of the millennium, fin-
ishing the whole with some of my own verses,
describing the glorious state, out of *Religious
Musings.*" He thus concludes the humorous
scene : " My taper man of lights listened
with perseverant and praiseworthy patience,
though, as I was afterwards told, on complain-
ing of certain gales that were not altogether
ambrosial, it was a melting day with him.
' And what, sir,' he said, after a short pause,
' might the cost be ? ' — ' Only four-pence,'
— (Oh ! how I felt the anti-climax, the abys-
mal bathos of that four-pence !) —' only four-
pence, sir, each number, to be published on
every eighth day.' — ' That comes to a deal of
money at the end of a year. And how much

did you say there was to be for the money?'
— 'Thirty-two pages, sir! large octavo, closely
printed.'—'Thirty and two pages? Bless me!
why, except what I does in a family way on
the Sabbath, that's more than I ever reads,
. sir! all the year round. I am as great a one,
as any man in Brummagem, sir! for liberty
and truth and all them sort of things, but as to
this, — no offense, I hope, sir, I must beg to
be excused.' "

Coleridge made but one more attempt in
person to get subscribers, and that is described,
in the tenth chapter of the *Biographia Literaria*, as amusingly as the first.

At Birmingham he preached twice to immense audiences. In a letter to his friend
Wade of Bristol he tells him : " My sermons
(in great part extempore) were preciously pep-
pered with politics. I have here at least
double the number of subscribers I expected."
Indeed, *The Watchman* might have been successful but for the procrastinating habits and
the constitutional inertness, as to outward
things, of Coleridge. Moreover, he was subject
to fits of deep melancholy, during which he
was like a man imprisoned who has no hope
of liberty.

From Lichfield, towards the close of the canvassing tour, he wrote to Wade a letter concluding thus characteristically :

" I verily believe no poor fellow's idea-pot ever bubbled up so vehemently with fears, doubts, and difficulties, as mine does at present. Heaven grant it may not boil over and put out the fire! I am almost heartless. My past life seems to me like a dream, a feverish dream — all one gloomy huddle of strange actions, and dim-discovered motives ; friendships lost by indolence, and happiness murdered by mis-managed sensibility. The present hour I seem in a quick-set hedge of embarrassments. For shame! I ought not to mistrust God ; but, indeed, to hope is far more difficult than to fear. Bulls have horns, lions have talons :

> " The fox and statesman subtle wiles ensure,
> The cit and polecat stink and are secure ;
> Toads with their venom, doctors with their drug,
> The priest and hedgehog in their robes are snug.
> Oh, Nature ! cruel stepmother and hard
> To thy poor naked, fenceless child, the bard !
> No horns but those by luckless Hymen worn,
> And those, alas ! not Amalthæa's horn !
> With aching feelings and with aching pride,
> He bears the unbroken blast on every side ;
> Vampire booksellers drain him to the heart,
> And scorpion critics cureless venom dart.
>   "S. T. C."

At Lichfield he would make no effort to get subscribers, because he might thereby injure the sale of *The Iris*, "the editor of which," he writes, "a very amiable and ingenious young man of the name of James Montgomery, is now in prison for a libel on a bloody-minded magistrate there. Of course I declined publicly advertising or disposing of *The Watchman* in that town."

On returning to Bristol Coleridge spent February in getting ready his first volume of poems. Mr. Cottle of Bristol had given him thirty guineas for the copyright. At the same time he was preparing the first number of *The Watchman*, to be issued on the 1st of March. And his wife was ill. On the 22d of February, 1796, he writes to his friend Cottle a plaintive, despondent, touching letter, which opens thus : "It is my duty and business to thank God for all his dispensations, and to believe them the best possible ; but, indeed, I think I should have been more thankful if he had made me a journeyman shoemaker instead of an author by trade." After a few lines he continues: "I am forced to write for bread — write the flights of poetic enthusiasm, when every minute I am hearing

a groan from my wife! Groans, and com-
plaints, and sickness! The present hour I am
in a quick-set hedge of embarrassment, and,
whichever way I turn, a thorn runs into me!
The future is cloud and thick darkness. Poverty, perhaps, and the thin faces of them that
want bread looking up to me! Nor is this all.
My happiest moments for composition are
broken in upon by the reflection that I must
make haste. 'I am too late.' 'I am already
months behind.' ' I have received my pay be-
forehand.' — O wayward and desultory spirit
of Genius, ill canst thou brook a taskmaster!
The tenderest touch from the hand of obliga-
tion wounds thee like a scourge of scorpi-
ons!"

The letter concludes as follows: " If I have
written petulantly, forgive me. God knows I
am sore all over. God bless you! and believe me that, setting gratitude aside, I love
and esteem you, and have your interest at
heart full as much as my own."

The Watchman mounted guard over the
public welfare punctually on the 1st of March.
On its score Coleridge soon began to receive
anonymous letters. One of these ran thus:
"Sir, I detest your principles; your prose I

think so so; but your poetry is so beautiful
that I take in your *Watchman* solely on account of it. In justice, therefore, to me and
some others of my stamp, I entreat you to give
us more verse, and less democratic scurrility.
Your admirer, not esteemer."

Alas! *The Watchman* kept its high watch
for hardly three months. With the tenth number it ceased to appear. Just before its decease Coleridge wrote to his friend Thomas
Poole : "*O Watchman, thou hast watched in
vain!* said the prophet Ezekiel, when, I suppose, he was taking a prophetic glimpse of my
sorrow-sallowed cheeks."

Poole was to Coleridge not only a sympathizing and generous, but an intellectually re-
sponsive, friend, to whom he pours out his
thoughts and feelings so confidentially and
freely that his letters to Poole have the frankness and fullness and the *naïveté* of a man
thinking aloud or speaking to himself. From
one written in November, 1796, the following
is an important passage : —

"I wanted such a letter as yours, for I am
very unwell. On Wednesday night I was
seized with an intolerable pain from my right
temple to the tip of my right shoulder, includ-

ing my right eye, cheek, jaw, and that side of
the throat. I was nearly frantic, and ran about
the house almost naked, endeavoring by every
means to excite sensation in different parts of
my body, and so to weaken the enemy by creating a division. It continued from one in the
morning till half-past five, and left me pale
and fainty. It came on fitfully, but not so vio-
lently, several times on Thursday, and began
severer threats towards night ; but I took between sixty and seventy drops of laudanum,
and sopped the Cerberus just as his mouth began to open. On Friday it only niggled, as if
the Chief had departed, as from a conquered
place, and merely left a small garrison behind,
or as if he had evacuated the Corrica, and a
few straggling pains only remained. But this
morning he returned in full force, and his name
is Legion. Giant-Fiend of a hundred hands,
with a shower of arrowy death-pangs he trans-
pierced me, and then he became a Wolf and
lay gnawing my bones ! — I am not mad, most
noble Festus ! but in sober sadness I have
suffered this day more bodily pain than I had
before a conception of. My right cheek has
certainly been placed with admirable exact-
ness under the focus of some invisible burn-

ing-glass, which concentrated all the rays of a Tartarean sun. My medical attendant decides it to be altogether nervous, and that it originates either in severe application, or excessive anxiety. My beloved Poole, in excessive anxiety I believe it might originate. I have a blister under my right ear, and I take twenty-five drops of laudanum every five hours, the ease and spirits gained by which have enabled me to write to you this flighty, but not exaggerating, account."

Here then was Coleridge's first acquaintance with this smiling sycophantic demon, masked in the guise of a helper. How many thousands of drunkards have been begotten by unsanctified prescriptions of alcohol in cases of disease! Certain constitutions are peculiarly liable to be thus permanently poisoned. Coleridge was of a lymphatic temperament. And when, in addition, we recollect how, in his tenth year, he was taken about by his uncle from tavern to tavern in London, during several weeks, " where," he relates, " I drank and talked and disputed as if I had been a man," it behooves us, when we come to the disabling effects of opium in Coleridge's middle life, to be liberal of that charity we owe to

5

all men, and to use an exceptional degree of forbearance towards one who was not stoutly organized and who was exceptionally afflicted and tempted.

The seeds of those agonizing neuralgic attacks may have been planted when, a child of six years, he lay out all night on the damp ground. On another occasion, several years later, while at Christ's Hospital, he swam across a stream in his clothes and let them dry on him. At no time of his life had Coleridge quite an average share of the homely virtue, prudence. He was better equipped with wings than with legs : he could soar to the region, and revel there, where broad visionary reason overlooks and rules human affairs, but he could not walk steadily among them, providing for the smaller wants of the day. In few superior men has the spirit been more clogged by the body than in Coleridge. Irksome to him were the stoopings, the declensions, that have to be made to meet the necessities of the bodily being. Of him might partly be said what was spoken of Joubert by one of his lady friends, "that he seemed to be a soul that by accident had met with a body and tries to make the best of it."

In this partnership between soul and body, not only is the soul the head of the firm, as furnishing the capital which gives credit and power to the house, but to it is due any popularity and acceptability the house enjoys. To his reach and liveliness of soul Coleridge owed not merely the significance and attractiveness of his writings, prose and verse, but also his personal fascination, which was always remarkable, and which, in these the days of his first failures, became the source of nourishing streams. The noble Thomas Poole, drawn to him by the charm of his genius and conversation, was serviceable to Coleridge in other ways than through the sympathy he gave the poet and thinker, rare and precious as was to Coleridge that sympathy. A little later the two brothers Wedgwood, inventors and prosperous manufacturers of a new tasteful delft ware, through admiration of Coleridge, bestowed on him an annuity of one hundred and fifty pounds, which continued many years, and the half of which he enjoyed till towards the end of his life. In that day one hundred and fifty pounds a year was a very substantial contribution to the housekeeping fund of a young married couple. Wordsworth began on a hundred pounds.

A few years later still, De Quincey, just come of age, moved by admiration of the genius and extraordinary mental powers of Coleridge, made him an anonymous gift of three hundred pounds, through the intermedium of a common friend, Cottle, the bookseller of Bristol. A most timely relief was this generous gift, for Coleridge was then much embarrassed and depressed, notwithstanding that a short time before he had received in one year eight hundred pounds as Secretary to the Governor of Malta.

A good story is told by Coleridge of himself and a Jew. More than usually annoyed one day in London by the nasal monotony of a crier of old clothes, he went up to him and said : " Pray, why can't you say Old Clothes as I do ? " The Jew stopped, and looking gravely at his reprover, said in a clear and even fine tone : " Sir, I can say Old Clothes as well as you can, but if you had to say so ten times a minute for an hour together, you would say *Ogh Clo* as I do :" and then walked on. So confounded was Coleridge by the justice of the retort, that he ran after the man, and gave him a shilling, the only one he had. That shilling being the last is as characteristic as

•the generous impulse to give it to the wronged
Jew. Money burned in Coleridge's pocket.
It may be doubted whether, with his organization, any probable provision — say an annuity
of four hundred pounds instead of one hundred and fifty pounds — would have secured
him against occasional pinching for want of
a guinea or a shilling. Some grandly gifted
men are irremediably thus constituted. Dan-
iel Webster was also a victim of this magnani-
mous impecuniosity, which has a noble air of
large-handedness in contrast with the minute
meannesses of avarice, but which closes the
hand to many a generous opportunity, and
constrains an honorable man to doings that
bring a blush to his cheek. Coleridge was a
rich-toned, sonorous, high-wrought harp, with
some of the strings incorrigibly unstrung.

IV.

NOTABLE years in the life of Coleridge were 1797 and 1798. In 1797 he took a house in Nether Stowey, near the Bristol Channel, and Wordsworth established himself at Alfoxden, a pleasant country-house among the Quantoc hills, in order to be near him.

The friendship between Goethe and Schiller was entered upon when Goethe was in his forty-fifth and Schiller in his thirty-fifth year, and, though begun at so comparatively late a period, was prolific of good to both. Close contact with a younger aspiring poet rekindled in Goethe his poetic fires, which for some time had been smoldering. Schiller's intellectual horizon was enlarged by the far outlook and experience of his friend, while his poetic aims gained in definiteness and fidelity. When Wordsworth and Coleridge became intimate friends Coleridge was in his twenty-sixth year, and Wordsworth two years older. To both the brilliant boundless realm of poetry was unfolding its unspeakable attractions. And so on the mind of his companion each beheld mirrored objects and vistas in this realm, the whole wondrous region was doubly illuminated. What Coleridge thought, twenty years later, of the poetic faculty and performance of Wordsworth is recorded in several successive chapters of the *Biographia Literaria*, chapters which embody some of the truest and highest criticism, and as profound an exposition of æsthetic principles as was ever written.

So intimate was at this time between Wordsworth and Coleridge interchange of thought, so cordial their association, so close their æsthetic concord, that they undertook to write a poem conjointly. Of this the impracticability showed itself at the very outset. In a great poet the current of inspiration flows from too individual a spring and with too strong a momentum to accommodate itself to the movement of another inspiration; and when that other is as fresh and vigorous as its own, the two poets at once discover that between them there can be no coöperation upon the same poem. When to talent more than to genius is due the efficiency of two poets, such coöperation may be successful. In Coleridge and Wordsworth genius used talent as its instrument; and it was owing to deficiency of talent in certain directions that Wordsworth's genius was not more effective.

This was the era of the *Lyrical Ballads*. If genius forbade the combining of their poetic forces for a joint achievement, by their contact and congenial converse the genius of each was enlivened and inflamed, and empowered for independent effort. Now it was that Coleridge produced the poems commented upon in the opening chapter. Of these poems a characteristic is their objectivity. The French Revolution, and the mental movement which engendered it, developed, stimulated individuality. The more susceptive the mind, the more liable was it to be rapt into this cyclone of thought and feeling, which promised to sweep away all barriers and obstructions to individual freedom. Poets were filled, inspired, by the promises of the time. In Wordsworth subjectivity took the form of sympathy for the poor, which was a broad and noble feature of the new spirit. In him this influence was facilitated by the republican and primitive habits of Cumberland and Westmoreland, where he was born and brought up. At the same time his intense self-consciousness made it easy, nay,

inevitable, for him to imbue his poetry with
his personality. On every page of Shelley,
who came two decades later, the noblest feature in the movement of the age is impressed,
in the form of fiery protest against tyranny, of
a deep yearning for emancipation. In Byron's
verse much of the restlessness and tumult of
the age finds expression ; but it is through the
strength of his egoism that he is the most subjective of the brilliant band of poets of that
upheaving period. His *Laras* and *Giaours* and
Childe Harolds are but superficially variegated
reduplications of himself.

Some people have not enough of disinterested sympathy, of generic breadth, to be able
to swing themselves beyond the circuit of their
individuality. They get at last to be imprisoned in themselves, — the most awful form of
solitary confinement. Byron is the poetic rep-
resentative of this self-entombed class. He
is the opposite of Shakespeare. Byron's personages are mirrors in which he sees himself ;
Shakespeare is himself a mirror, in which his
personages are reflected. Shakespeare is in
all his personages because all humanity is in
him. How unlike Byron is to Shakespeare
let himself declare. In the Introduction to

Sardanapalus is this sentence : " You will find
all this very *un*like Shakespeare ; and so much
the better in one sense, for I look upon him to
be the worst of models, though the most extraordinary of writers.   It has been my object
to be as simple and severe as Alfieri, and I
have broken down the poetry as nearly as I
could to common language."   Here is subjectivity with a vengeance !   That "*un*like Shakespeare " came from a thought, and not a momentary thought, of likeness.   Shakespeare
is not called the greatest of poets, but the
most extraordinary of writers.   The greatest
of poets is another Englishman.   To reject
Shakespeare as a bad model, and take the
juiceless Alfieri as a good one !   Were this a
study of Byron, pages of comment might be
written on this one characteristic, most significant passage.

The opposite of Byron in feeling towards
Shakespeare, Coleridge had not the presumption to be jealous of the mightiest of poets.
He kindled his own great faculties to their
brightest to pour light upon the master's page
in rich, most discriminative eulogy.   Straining
to make admiration come up to Shakespeare's
unparalleled performance, he coined a grand

new epithet to be applied solely to him, — *myriad-minded.*

Like Shakespeare himself, and unlike Byron, was Coleridge in the objectivity of his mind's movement. His was not a nature that is self-busied while depicting imaginary persons and scenes. In presence of large or lively themes, the self in him was effaced. In its poetic flights, his imagination freed itself from personality. This was not owing to the largeness of his intellect, or to the power of his poetic imagination, but to the sobriety of his self-seeking impulses. Coleridge was the opposite of a self-sufficient man ; there was no assumption, no arrogance, in him. In Wordsworth there was, and in Byron inordinate vanity ; and these were largely the sources of their subjectivity as poets, — a subjectivity differing in quality and degree in the two, being more intense in Byron, saturating most of his poems with himself, while imbuing many of Wordsworth's with the spirit of the times.

Now in *Christabel, The Ancient Mariner,* and *Kubla Khan* there is not a trace, neither of the yearnings and aspirations of the French Revolution period, nor of personal characteristics. They belong to no age or country ; their personages and conditions, while warmly human, have on them no soilure of the earth; they are woven out of poetic sunbeams. They are creations of imaginative potency, more sparkling with the ethereal essence of poetic life than any product from any of his great contemporaries, except Shelley.

The friendship between Wordsworth and Coleridge led to their making a trip to Germany together. Coleridge had at times in his mind the vision of a select school to be kept by him. To accomplish himself more thoroughly for this duty was part of his motive for going to Germany and Göttingen. The school never came to be more than a scheme. Coleridge was a man of unexecuted projects in practical life, in philosophy, and in poetry. The difference between the ease and rapidity of imaginary work — especially to a mind so copious and creative as his — and the labor and slowness of execution, the difference between building in the brain and building on the ground, was never more distinctly exhibited than in the case of Coleridge. But, unlike most visionaries, there was solidity as well as splendor in his thoughts. So stored are these with learning and knowledge, and, what is bet-

ter than either, with wisdom, that his volumes
are among the most valuable, as well as the
most brilliant, in our language.

I was at Göttingen a quarter of a century
later than Coleridge. Professor and Librarian
Benecke, my very capable teacher of German,
then a man of nearly sixty, told me that when
the *Confessions of an Opium-Eater* appeared,
he attributed it to Coleridge, because when at
Göttingen he took opium. The terrible drug,
taken at first as medicine, transformed from a
soother of pain into a syren of destruction, had
now laid its enduring spell upon another illustrious victim.

Benecke related how Coleridge, shortly after
his arrival, would declaim in German one of
Klopstock's odes, mystifying his English fellow-
students into the belief that he had mastered
it. But Coleridge, before going to Göttingen,
had passed several weeks at Ratzeburg, daily
busied, no doubt, with dictionary and grammar.

Before he went to Germany, Coleridge, as
we have seen, had written some of his best
poems. Wordsworth thought that by his visit
to Germany he was drawn astray from poetry
into metaphysics. By learning German he

was enabled to read Kant and Schelling; but it appears that he did not give in to the study of them until some years later. Superior as well as inferior men are liable to all kinds of influences, sometimes injurious influences; but is a man of the high poetic originality, the deep inwardness, of Coleridge likely to be injuriously affected, to the degree that Wordsworth affirms, by external attractions? We have seen how, even in his boyhood, he became absorbed in speculative thinkers. He had a metaphysical as well as a poetic genius. To regret that he did not write more *Christabels* and *Ancient Mariners* were not only idle, but ungrateful. Few writers have left to their fellow-men so much that is good as Coleridge has. Not only should we thankfully hug what he has given, without grumbling that he gave no more, but it were perhaps wise to conclude that he gave us all he had to give. A lesser poet could not have written *Christabel*, from defect of poetic imagination. Coleridge left *Christabel* unfinished, from defect of other qualities than poetic imagination. Had he possessed these qualities to the degree he did that, they would have rounded him to a superhuman perfection. Some of his inherent inevitable human deficiency lay behind the opium and lifted it to his lips.

The first fruit of his German studies was a translation of Schiller's *Wallenstein*, a trilogy, the three parts being *Wallenstein's Camp, The Piccoluomini*, and *Wallenstein's Death*. The *Camp* is introductory, is written in rhyme, and depicts the heterogeneous character and the lawlessness of Wallenstein's army, together with its devotion to and belief in its General. This Coleridge did not translate on account of the difficulty of rendering it with fidelity and at the same time with spirit. *The Piccoluomini* and *Wallenstein's Death* are two separate plays, each of five acts. Without aiming to detract from the great merit of Schiller's masterpiece, I cannot but think that, had the two plays been compressed into one under the name of *Wallenstein*, a more intense, a higher and more poetical, work of Art might have been produced.

Schiller has the rare good fortune to have his greatest drama translated into a cognate tongue by one who, himself a poet, executed his labor of love with the zeal of genius. Coleridge is, indeed, superior, both as poet and as thinker, to Schiller himself. The translation, made from manuscript, was published in London simultaneously with the original in Germany. Coleridge was probably hurried, in order to be up to time. There are frequent marks of haste, especially in the want of condensation, and in the use of polysyllabic Latin-English, instead of monosyllabic Saxon-English. The translation had hardly any sale, and so Coleridge had no opportunity for remedying the defects caused by haste.

V.

WHEN Coleridge, at the close of the last century, returned from Germany, armed with a new language and a new literature, he was in his twenty-ninth year, he was in the bloom of an uncommonly rich young manhood. Into the lively arena, where great principles were then interlocked in a death-grapple, no man in England of that wakeful period brought more mental force, more intellectual accomplishment. Mr. Stuart, the active, able conductor of *The Morning Post*, for which paper Coleridge was engaged to write, declared, many years after, in reviewing his connection with Coleridge at that period: "To write the leading paragraph of a newspaper I would prefer Coleridge to Mackintosh, Burke, or any man I ever heard of. His observations not only were confirmed by good sense, but displayed extensive knowledge, deep thought, and well-grounded foresight ; they were so brilliantly ornamented, so classically delightful. They were the writings of a scholar, a gentleman, and a statesman, without personal sarcasm or illiberality of any kind. But when Coleridge wrote in his study without being pressed, he wandered and lost himself. He should always have had the printer's devil at his elbow with *Sir, the printers want copy.*"

Irresolution caused by bad health is not enough to account for the failures of Coleridge. He seems to have been deficient in what the phrenologists call *concentrativeness*, the faculty of holding the intellect continuously to its task. Opium, no doubt, had something to do with the inaptitude for steady work. The pretended cure for disease became the generator of worse disease. The want of will to resist the fascination of the disguised demon gave this demon the power to dethrone an ill-guarded will. On another occasion, a few years later, speaking of what Coleridge wrote for *The Courier* about the war in Spain, Mr. Stuart said: "Could Coleridge have written the leading paragraph daily his services would have been invaluable, but an occasional essay could produce little effect."

From a successful conductor of London daily newspapers this is strong testimony as to the capability of Coleridge. To those who

now read his prose-volumes, with that high
enjoyment imparted by the pages of Plato,
drawing from him the calm inspiration of profound and spiritual thoughtfulness, it seems
almost incredible that the same man was able
to produce, in their most effective potency,
those stirring paragraphs best fitted to spur
men's minds to instant action.

In 1804 Coleridge, on account of ill health,
and to visit a friend, made a voyage to Malta.
Here he became intimate with a superior
man, Sir Alexander Ball, Governor of Malta,
who made Coleridge for a time his secretary.
From Malta he went to Rome, where he met
Allston. Congenial spirits were these two,
both splendidly gifted, richly poetical as well
as intellectual, and both spiritually-minded.
Two or three years before he died, Allston, in
his studio at Cambridgeport, on my mention-
ing Coleridge, spoke of him with reverence as
well as intense admiration : " The greatest
man that ever I accosted." In uttering these
words his voice fell and his manner grew almost solemn, as though for the moment his
vision had before it his great friend. Other
eminent contemporaries who came in contact
with him (and the closer the contact the

stronger the impression) were similarly impressed by his presence and converse. Charles
Lamb, who admired not less than he loved
Coleridge, called him, with Lamb's peculiar
humor, "an archangel a little damaged." The
scholarly, eloquent De Quincey, with a dash
of that polished exaggeration into which he is
occasionally seduced, speaks of him as "the
largest and most spacious intellect, the subtlest
·and most comprehensive, in my judgment, that
has yet existed amongst men." Wordsworth
says: "The only wonderful man I ever knew
was Coleridge."

Coleridge quitted Rome suddenly, on a con-
fidential hint that Napoleon had ordered his
arrest. That such an order was given has been
denied, on the ground that the King-crush-
ing Emperor would not have condescended
to notice the then unknown private Englishman. But Napoleon was as minute as he was
unscrupulous in the instrumentalities of his
despotism, and had all the hate and dread in-
stinctive to despots, of independent thinkers
and bold men of genius, — a feeling deepened
in this case by his hatred of England. His
spies and informers were everywhere. In 1802
and 1803 Coleridge wrote in *The Morning Post*

• against him, and we know how watchful Napoleon was, especially in those years of transition, of the London newspapers, and how sensitive to their comments. The order may not have been issued, but the reason cited above for its non-issue is assuredly unsound.

Coleridge, acting on the hint given him, made his way to Leghorn, where he took passage in an American vessel bound to England. They were chased by a French cruiser, and the captain obliged Coleridge to throw over board his papers, — a precautionary measure not creditable to the captain of the American merchantman, and one less likely to be resorted to in 1876 than in 1806. Coleridge thus lost all the notes he had taken at Rome.

On returning to England he went back to reside at Keswick, where he had left his family on starting for Malta. At this period he was again much with Wordsworth, who then had a cottage at Grasmere, thirteen miles from Keswick. To one so poetically gifted, so richly endowed, so highly cultivated, this decade of his life, between his thirty-fifth and forty-fifth years, ought to have been, and might have been, a period of joyous mental activity and productiveness and manful expansion. But

Coleridge was restless, unhappy, irresolute, depressed. For years he was the sorrowful, abject slave to opium. By this accursed habit his health and spirits were blasted, his plans frustrated, his undertakings baffled, his usefulness crippled, his conscience seared. Engaged by the Royal Society to deliver a course of lectures on Poetry and Art, the intelligent, refined audience had sometimes to be dismissed on the plea of the sudden illness of the lecturer. The performance of his duties at the *Courier* office, where he was engaged to write, was irregular.

Coleridge, clogged in his movement by this impure habit, is as though an eagle, snatching from the ground a polecat, should become so infatuated with its odor as not to be able to drop it when he found his flight impeded. — This starts a reflection. The eagle, though by his size and strength, by the elevation and range of his winged sweep, the first among the fowls of the air, is a bird of prey. So there are human beings, and some among the strongest, who are men of prey. Foremost among these was Bonaparte, and therefore most fitting it was that he should adopt as his Imperial emblem the eagle, borrowing it from Rome.

Rome, as a conquering nation, is to be classed among animals of prey. Thence the eagle is not a suitable emblem for the United States, for we are not a conquering nation. Our aims are other than the ravenous devouring of neighbors, and, to bring our national emblem into harmony with our nature and principles, we should discard a carnivorous bird of prey, leaving the eagle to Prussia and Austria and Russia, all of whom have with a sound instinct chosen it ; leaving, too, to England her prowling, voracious lion. — To return to Coleridge, from whom this eagle-flight has borne us away.

Through *The Watchman*, a dozen years earlier, he had had proof of his unfitness to conduct a paying periodical work, — an unsuitableness due to the deep alternations in his health and spirits, to his procrastinating habits, to the elevated range and ideal aim of his thoughts. Untaught by this trial, about the year 1810 he issued the first number of *The Friend*, the object of which was to present and unfold first principles in philosophy, politics, ethics, literature.

The wide and lofty scope of *The Friend* is an exponent of its projector. The mental life of

Coleridge was in the deep places and the high places of being. So impressed was he with the power and grandeur of generative ideas, so possessed by them, so intimate with them, that he was ever striving to share them with others, to imbue the educated and thoughtful with them, and thus elevate mankind through the force and beauty there is in fundamental divine principles. His ascensions and ranges were like those of the mountain-haunting, sky-piercing eagle, but alas! unlike those of the eagle, his were not predatory, and brought no food to his eyric.

It were easy to wish that he had been more earthly-minded, had practiced a little more worldly prudence. By this deficiency his family and contemporary friends could not but be pained and provoked. They, no doubt, did what they could to remedy it; but for us, his posterity, the heirs of rich legacies, it becomes us to be reserved and thankful. To throw reproachfully, even at a living fellow-man, the commonplaces about duty is not a profitable proceeding, is, indeed, immoral, weakening the thrower through assumption and self-flattery, and irritating rather than correcting the delinquent. Moments there are when the assertion of moral principles is appropriate and imperative ; but this is not one of them. The great and good Coleridge is not a subject for shallow rebuke. His infirmities affected those nearest to him in an indirect negative way, however potently ; directly and aggressively he never injured a human being, save himself. He was not ambitious, not greedy of power, and thence he was not touched by that curse to so many of his tribe, envy and jealousy. In his undertakings he was moved by aspiration after the true and good, not by worldly desires.

Leaving out of view the disabling effects of opium, it may be doubted whether Coleridge had enough of practical talent and prudence, of daily provident outlook, to supply the ever recurrent demands of a family. To himself this inability was a source of anxiety, depression, self-reproach. On the margin of Lamb's copy of *Dramatic Scenes* by Proctor, at the end of an acute and generous criticism of Proctor's verse, he makes this reflection : " Oh ! for such a man worldly prudence is transfigured into the highest spiritual duty ! How generous is self-interest in him, whose true self is all that is good and hopeful in all ages, as far as the language of Spenser, Shakespeare, and Milton

shall become the mother-tongue." And then
he adds in a separate paragraph :

"A map of the road to Paradise, drawn in
Purgatory, on the confines of Hell, by S. T. C.
July 30th, 1819."

Made aware by these startling words to what
a depth of soul-suffering so great a being may
be brought by his own acts, we can only heave
a sigh of sympathy for the illustrious victim,
and reflect on the fallibility of man.

Whoever would know Coleridge — and to
know him well is something like a privilege —
should not dwell on the picture drawn by De
Quincey when, about the year 1807, Coleridge
was living at the *Courier* office, often "struggling with pain, his lips baked with feverish
heat and often black in color," when, in short,
his great soul was vexed and shadowed by the
vices of the body; but should take in the image of him that is presented by Henry Nelson
Coleridge in the *Table Talk* on such a day as
the 24th of June, 1827, when he "talked a volume of criticism which, printed *verbatim* as he
spoke it, would make the reputation of any
other man but himself. The sun was setting
behind Caen wood, and the calm of the evening was so exceedingly deep that it arrested

Mr. Coleridge's attention. He left off talking, and fell into an almost trance-like state for ten minutes, whilst contemplating the beautiful prospect before us. His eyes swam in tears, his head inclined a little forward, and there was a slight uplifting of the fingers, which seemed to tell me he was in prayer. I was awe-stricken, and remained absorbed in looking at the man in forgetfulness of external nature, when he recovered himself and after a word or two fell by some secret link of association upon Spenser's poetry."

The Friend, as a periodical publication, was a failure ; and Coleridge, being not merely editor but publisher, lost money by it. As issued afterwards in three volumes, containing profound disquisitions, illustrated and enriched with apt and various knowledge, *The Friend* is a casket full of precious thoughts. Take this as a sample (from page 132 of Marsh's American edition of 1831) : " The understanding of the higher brutes has only organs of outward sense, and consequently sees material objects only ; but man's understanding has moreover organs of inward sense, and therefore the power of acquainting itself with invisible realities or spiritual objects." To thoughtful schol-

ars this is valuable; but think of a man trying
to make "the pot boil" with such fuel. Or
read, on page 410, a long passage on Nature,
Idea, Intuition, and Plato. Truly one who
sought to meet daily family expenses through
the means of such material was infatuated
with high philosophy and abstruse thinking.
There are, to be sure, many practical, easily
intelligible sentences and pages, like this, for
example: "Like arms without hearts are the
widest maxims of *prudence* disjoined from those
feelings which flow forth from *principle* as from
a fountain." The writings of Coleridge are
ballasted with common sense, and his common
sense is the more solid because strengthened
by the ideal, and because his nature was large
and lofty enough to furnish sound ideals to
draw from.

A man's life is multiplied, enlarged, ennobled, by interest in his fellow-men, by devotion
to those spiritual and intellectual principles
that advance and uplift mankind. Thus am-
plified and elevated was Coleridge. The high
and wide range of his intellect and his sympathies is exemplified in *The Friend*, the first,
chronologically, of his prose works. In this,
as in those that follow it, we have everywhere

a clear, strong, brilliant mind disinterestedly in earnest. The thought is vivid, the expression apt. He never deals in decorated or polished commonplace. In the writings of Coleridge, through his effective intellectual endowment, especially through his sure perception of likeness, the associative power is uncommonly active, and thence rare vivacity and attractiveness are imparted to his printed page. This, too, was a chief source of his fascinating speech, thought suggesting thought in an endless series of concatenated imaginations, which his poetic sensibility enfolded in its radiance. And of his pages a crowning virtue it is that they all tend to the spiritualization of man.

The mind of Coleridge was so copious and fluent that upon the margins of volumes he was reading it overflowed in rapid, pithy comment. Charles Lamb liked to lend him books, they came back, he said, so enriched. Many of these *marginalia* have been collected into four volumes of *Literary Remains*, edited by his nephew, Henry Nelson Coleridge. These volumes are a treasury of critical judgments on an endless variety of subjects, literary, philosophical, theological, all of them derived from or grounded on generative principles.

Whether you accept them or not, they feed
your thought with suggestion or stimulation.
In them is the pulse of thoughtful life, the
gleam of genial light. The most valuable
chapters are the reports of lectures on Literature and Art and on Shakespeare. The notes
on Shakespeare are a lively stream of sympathetic commentary, flowing from heights which
stretch into the infinite and invisible, and re-
plenished, invigorated, by springs that rise up
from the practical along men's daily walks.
These springs are deeper and these heights
loftier than most men have access to, and so
all critics and commentators on Shakespeare,
even the most accomplished, fail not to look
into Coleridge to get assurance of their success as interpreters of the profoundest of poets.

From the coincidence between certain principles and judgments put forth by Coleridge
and those found in Schlegel's lectures on *Dramatic Literature*, it was inferred by some,
whose wish was father to the thought, that
Coleridge had borrowed without acknowledg-
ment from Schlegel. In the following valuable letter, written in 1818, Coleridge disposes
of this calumny :

"My next Friday's lecture will, if I do not

grossly flatter-blind myself, be interesting, and
the points of view not only original, but new
to the audience. I make this distinction, because sixteen or rather seventeen years ago I
delivered eighteen lectures on Shakespeare, at
the Royal Institution ; three fourths of which
appeared at that time startling paradoxes, although they have since been adopted even by
men who then made use of them as proofs
of my flighty and paradoxical turn of mind ;
all tending to prove that Shakespeare's judgment was, if possible, still more wonderful
than his genius ; or rather, that the contra-
distinction itself between judgment and genius
rested on an utterly false theory. This and
its proofs and grounds have been — I should
not have said adopted, but produced as their
own legitimate children by some, and by others the merit of them attributed to a foreign
writer, whose lectures were not given orally
till two years after mine, rather than to their
countryman ; though I dare appeal to the most
adequate judges, as Sir George Beaumont, the
Bishop of Durham, Mr. Sotheby, and afterwards to Mr. Rogers and Lord Byron, whether
there is one single principle in Schlegel's work
(which is not an admitted drawback from its

merits) that was not established and applied
in detail by me. Plutarch tells us that egotism is a venial fault in the unfortunate, and
justifiable in the calumniated," etc.

In another letter, written in 1819, he thus
recurs to this subject: " The coincidence between my lectures and those of Schlegel was
such and so close that it was fortunate for my
moral reputation that I had not only from five
to seven hundred ear-witnesses that the passages had been given by me at the Royal
Institution two years before Schlegel commenced his lectures at Vienna, but that notes
had been taken of these by several ladies and
men of high rank."

More even than most men of genius Coleridge was a target for the shafts of envious
or ignorant detraction, embittered in England
during the first decades of the present century
by the gall of party-politics. Thus Jeffrey, in
the *Edinburgh Review*, called *Christabel* " a
mixture of raving and driveling." Now, neither Jeffrey nor any of his coadjutors, however
great their merits (and their merits were great,
for the permanent breach they made in the
Chinese wall of old abuses, and the example
they set of bold discussion), not one of them

had the fineness of faculty or the winged rate
and quality of motion required to reach the
poetic atmosphere where such a genuinely
new poem·was breathed forth.

Christabel Coleridge drew out of his spirituality, exalted by an exquisite poetic aspiration. The clever company of early Edinburgh
Reviewers were not a spiritually-minded set :
the good work they had to do required grosser
material and coarser tools than those with
which Christabels are conceived and con-
structed. Jeffrey, their chief critic of verse,
could appreciate Scott, but not Wordsworth
and Coleridge. Towards them, from spiritual
and poetic deficiencies, he was unjust, and
from self-complacency he gave impertinent utterance to his injustice, himself hardly aware
that he was impertinent. Among critics and
would-be critics Jeffrey will always have followers as self-sufficient as he was, cultivated
but not poetically-minded men who have more
ambition than insight, much more self-admi-
ration than modesty. And the shallowest of
this class will deal in the easy, graceless
method of scoff, just as by the Edinburgh Reviewers was fastened upon the three poet-
friends, Wordsworth, Coleridge, and Southey,

7

the preposterous misnomer *the Lake School.*
You will hear it now and then applied to them
at this late day, so pertinaciously will a nick-
name stick. The three differed in their poetic
principles as well as practice, and agreed only
in one thing, says Mr. Shairp, " their opposition to the hard and unimaginative spirit
which was then the leading characteristic of
the *Edinburgh Review.*"

Political rancor, in stormy times, sprinkled
wormwood in the ink of whig critics when
writing of these three, especially Coleridge,
who was acknowledged to be a powerful political writer ; but he was a political writer who
wrote like a philosopher, not like a partisan.
In 1800 Coleridge was with Fox in opposing
the war with France, but when he sagacious-
ly discerned, as Bonaparte unfolded himself,
that he was an unscrupulous, grasping despot,
he separated himself from the eloquent whig
leader. The self-justification of Coleridge for
going over to the tory side is complete. He
passed over to the tories, he says, " only in
the sense in which all patriots did so at that
time, by refusing to accompany the whigs
in their almost perfidious demeanor towards
Napoleon. Anti-ministerial they styled their

policy, but it was really anti-national. It was
exclusively in relation to the great feud with
Napoleon that I adhered to the tories. But
because this feud was so capital, so earth-shak-
ing, that it occupied all hearts, and all the
councils of Europe, suffering no other question almost to live in the neighborhood, hence
it happened that he who joined the tories in
this was regarded as their ally in everything.
Domestic politics were then in fact forgotten."

In more ways than one Coleridge suffered
for his unworldliness. The world loves world-
lings : it erects statues to ambitious public
self-seekers. To the world an idealist is hateful, partly because it cannot understand him,
but chiefly because he is a reproach to its
grossness and stolidity. The world is busy
with petty interests; Coleridge dealt in large
principles. He was ever looking beyond the
present, either backward or forward. He had
no aptness for superficiality : the world's work
is, most of it, necessarily on the surface.
Coleridge was a meditater, not an actor. He
was, to be sure, an exquisite artist as well as a
deep thinker ; but his artist-work was too delicate for the daily market. By the originality
of his genius he opened a road which enabled

Scott and Byron to cultivate the more pros-
perously their fields.· Them the immediate
public rewarded with guineas by the thousands ; him it left to starve.

Coleridge was always pecuniarily pinched,
and those who love and admire him are pained
when they think what extremities of indigence
he might have suffered but for the annuity of
the generous Wedgwoods. Towards the latter end of his life he enjoyed a pension from
the Crown, but of this, during his very last
years, when from grievous sickness he needed
it most, he was deprived, through the mean-
ness of some cruel adviser of the new King,
William IV.

VI.

In literature poetry is supreme, aiming to reach the quintessence of being, to make perceptible the very aroma of thought and life. And, as to divulge and present the essential nature of men and things is the purpose of all high literature, in its every department should be active that creative power which at its flood swells into poetry. The orator, the historian, the critic, the philosopher, the essayist, each fails to swing up to the height of his theme, to outfill the capability of his subject, unless his pulse be enlivened by draughts of the same breath that immortalizes *Hamlet* and *Faust*. That his work be not tame and unprofitable it must be illuminated by light from the beautiful. From this poetic source he gets a clearer insight, a readier mastery.

Now Coleridge was philosopher, essayist, critic, and, in his social monologues, an irresistible orator. And these diverse fields, through his rare competence to work them, had for him such attraction that they drew him from a full culture of the most fruitful of all literary fields, from a field in which his genius proved itself so generative. Or was it that his vein of poetry, genuine, rich, and refined, was neither broad nor thick ? Or was the ardor wherewith every poet plies his gift somewhat damped by outside opinion ? Coleridge was, as Wordsworth said, a wonderful man. He was a giant with one arm paralyzed, a sun with deep spots in it that dimmed its radiance. Possibly, but for the crippling contradictions in him, but for his unmanning weaknesses, his many-sided splendor would have been too dazzling.

What a curse opium was to him no one knew so well as himself. Whoever would reproach Coleridge, let him pause. If he is one to value what was great and good in this eminent man, his reproaches will turn into tears of sympathy after he shall have read these sentences written by Coleridge to his friend Wade : " In the one crime of opium, what crimes have I not made myself guilty of ? Ingratitude to my Maker ; and to my benefactors injustice ; and unnatural cruelty to my poor children. . . . . After my death, I earnestly entreat that a full and unqualified narrative of my wretchedness, and its guilty cause, may be made public, that at least some little good may be effected by the direful example."

One of the most genuine, ever fresh and delightful, of Coleridge's poems is *Youth and Age*. Written before he had entered his fortieth year, it is a plaint that youth is gone and age is come ; but it is not at all a wail, it is, I should say, more imaginative than personal. I make room for a third of it :

> " Flowers are lovely ; Love is flower-like :
> Friendship is a sheltering tree ;
> Oh the joys that came down shower-like,
> Of Friendship, Love, and Liberty,
>   Ere I was old !
> Ere I was old ? Ah, woeful *ere !*
> Which tells me Youth 's no longer here !
> O Youth ! for years so many and sweet,
> 'T is known that you and I were one ;
> I 'll think it but a fond deceit —
> It cannot be that thou art gone ! "

Kindly, tender, affectionate, not despondent by nature, neither restless with ambitious schemes, nor cast down by ambition's disappointments, with immense and various intellectual means, Coleridge had it in him to be happy, cheerful, and successful. But, like many others, and in a greater degree than most, he was a joint victim of circumstances and

himself. Men of mere talent are much less
liable to be injured by circumstances than men
of sensibility and genius, especially of poetic
genius. The world is a prosaic world. In its
daily doings and aspects it shows little of the
poetry it is capable of. It does not know, or
care, how to cherish and help men of creative
mind. Sometimes it fondles and spoils them.
Neither in his childhood, his boyhood, nor his
youth, had Coleridge the affectionate further-
ance, the sentimental support, the sympathetic
guidance, which a large sensitive nature needs,
if it is to be unfolded adequately to its endow-
ments and capabilities. Great men make circumstances; but boys and youths who are to
become great men are, on account of that very
latent power and in proportion to its strength,
exposed to be diverted and partially thwarted
by meagre or perverse circumstances.

Coleridge was not a man of worldly ambi-
tions; he was a man of intellectual and spiritual aspirations. Nevertheless, like other
gifted natures, he had his lower moods, his
moments of downward solicitation. In the re-
bound from one of these he probably penned
the well-known lines called *Complaint and
Reply.* These lines are a perpetual rebuke,

warning, and encouragement to genuine men
of letters :

> " How seldom, friend ! a good great man inherits
> Honor or wealth, with all his worth and pains !
> It sounds like stories from the land of spirits,
> If any man obtain that which he merits,
> Or any merit that which he obtains.
> For shame, dear friend ! renounce this canting strain !
> What wouldst thou have a good great man obtain ?
> Place — titles — salary — a gilded chain —
> Or throne of corses which his sword hath slain ?
> Greatness and goodness are not means, but ends !
> Hath he not always treasures, always friends,
> The good great man ? — three treasures, love, and light,
> And calm thoughts, regular as infant's breath ;
> And three firm friends, more sure than day and night —
> Himself, his Maker, and the angel Death."

Kubla Khan, The Ancient Mariner, and
Christabel — new beings begotten on the
brain of genius — are fragrant with subtle
meanings, penetrated by refined flames that
impart to every limb poetic life, and hang
around the whole an unquenchable luminousness. The poems he wrote in middle life have
more substance and a more direct bearing on
daily human affairs. If less ethereal than
these famous three, they are not less spiritual.
The controlling, the generative power of the
soul is an ever-present thought with Cole-

ridge. Of this the following lines from the
ode on *Dejection* is a happy illustration :

> " And would we aught behold of higher worth,
> Than that inanimate cold world allowed
> To the poor, loveless, ever anxious crowd,
>   Ah ! from the soul itself must issue forth
> A light, a glory, a fair luminous cloud
>   Enveloping the earth —
> And from the soul itself must there be sent
>   A sweet and potent voice, of its own birth,
> Of all sweet sounds the life and element ! "

The fidelity of Coleridge's intuitions to the
divinest demands of human nature, and the
prolific union in him of moral and poetical
sensibility, are nowhere more distinctly presented than in his poem entitled *Love, Hope,
and Patience in Education :*

> " O'er wayward childhood wouldst thou hold firm rule,
>   And sun thee in the light of happy faces ;
>   Love, Hope, and Patience, these must be thy graces,
>   And in thine own heart let them first keep school.
>   For as old Atlas on his broad neck places
>   Heaven's starry globe, and there sustains it, — so
>   Do these upbear the little world below
>   Of education, — Patience, Love, and Hope.
>   Methinks, I see them grouped, in seemly show,
>   The straightened arms upraised, the palms aslope,
>   And robes that, touching as adown they flow,
>   Distinctly blend, like snow embossed in snow.
>   Oh, part them never ! If Hope prostrate lie,
>   Love too will sink and die.

But Love is subtle, and doth proof derive
From her own life that Hope is yet alive ;
And bending o'er with soul-transfusing eyes,
And the soft murmurs of the mother Love,
Woos back the fleeting spirit and half-supplies ;
Thus Love repays to Hope what Hope first gave to Love,
Yet haply there will come a weary day,
   When, overtasked, at length
Both Love and Hope beneath the load give way.
Then with a statue's smile, a statue's strength,
Stands the mute sister, Patience, nothing loth,
And both supporting does the work of both."

An able critic in the *London Quarterly Review* for July, 1863, in an article on "Coleridge as a Poet," commenting on this poem, asks : "Can any other poem of this century be cited in which, within so small a compass, there is so wide a range ? "

The tragedy of *Remorse*, written in his first period, was accepted at Drury Lane Theatre in 1813, partly owing to the good offices of Lord Byron, at that time one of the directors of Drury Lane. *Remorse* had a run of twenty nights. This success encouraged Coleridge to write, and offer to Drury Lane, another tragedy, *Zapolya*, which was rejected. The best and brightest of Coleridge is not in his dramas. The acceptance and preparation of *Remorse* brought him into personal intercourse with

Byron, of whose countenance he gives this vivid portraiture : " If you had seen Lord Byron you could scarcely disbelieve him. So beautiful a countenance I scarcely ever saw ; his teeth so many stationary smiles ; his eyes the open portals of the sun — things of light, and made for light; and his forehead, so ample, and yet so flexible, passing from marble smoothness into a hundred wreaths and lines and dimples, correspondent to the feelings and sentiments he is uttering."

In 1816, after desperate but ineffectual struggles against the tyranny of opium, he voluntarily put himself under the control of Dr. Gilman, of Highgate, and took up his abode with him. Dr. and Mrs. Gilman proved to be kind, appreciative friends. Through their tender, watchful care the curse of opium was lifted from his soul. Beneath their roof he lived for eighteen years, until his death.

The mind of Coleridge was multifold. It had pinions, and it was armed with blades; it could soar, and it could delve ; it was poetical and philosophical, it was critical and creative. It was moved to embody the beautiful and to penetrate the abstruse. During his latter years he strove to dig deeper into the mines of metaphysics and theology, whose subtle problems he had sought to solve in his younger years.

The first direction given, even to a mind of largest mold, is sometimes due to what is called chance. Hartley had been a member of Jesus College, Cambridge, where Coleridge had rooms, and the upper atmosphere of Cambridge was imbued with his philosophy, whose principles, being derived from Locke, were materialistic. With these principles Coleridge. became infected so strongly that he named his first-born son Hartley. But no mind of full rich endowment can finally rest in philosophical doctrines so insufficient ; and so Coleridge, before he went to Germany, was, by the movement of his own higher mental wants, drawn upward towards a wider, cleaner track. His consciousness prompted him to infer that man were an abject creature, a mere earthling, if only through the senses and experience he got all his knowledge. He felt that within the mind itself there must be an originating life. The Transcendental philosophy confirmed this consciousness, demonstrating the existence of *a priori* conceptions independent of experience. If Kant did not absolutely reveal to Coleridge a new domain in the realm of mind, he laid bare the divisions of that realm with so much comparative clearness, that with his support and that of Schelling Coleridge gave his thought freer play in the region of metaphysics and speculative philosophy.

In a note to the concluding chapter of the *Biographia Litcraria*, Coleridge exclaims : " Poor unlucky Metaphysics ! and what are they ? A single sentence expresses the object and thereby the contents of this science : KNOW THYSELF. And so shalt thou know God, so far as is permitted to a creature, and in God all things. Surely, there is a strange, nay, rather a too natural, aversion in many to know themselves."

Was there ever penned deeper, greater, wiser sentences than these ? In a few lines what insight, what concentrated truth ! To know thyself were to hold in thy hand a key to that richest and most roomy of palaces, the mental constitution of man, and thereby have a clew to all that is within the ken of the human mind. We should be walking firmly, with sure hope, on the road to the solution of deepest problems, of those inclosed in metaphysics, in theology, in politics, in philosophy, in æsthetics. Thus armed, Coleridge could have cut his way through what he calls "the holy jungle of transcendental metaphysics."

But, like most other metaphysical thinkers, he took such delight in his own subjective mental activities that he could not gather up his intellectual forces for an unbiassed deliberation upon certain startling objective phenomena then lately laid bare, and thus seize their immense significance.

That there is a close connection between brain and mind, especially intellectual mind, has always been vaguely acknowledged, or, rather, indistinctly felt. Toward the end of the last century, Dr. Gall, a physician of Vienna, proved, by a thoroughly Baconian method, not only that there is a connection, close and indissoluble, between them, but that the brain is the indispensable organ of every kind of mental power ; and further, that, instead of being one single organ, it is a congeries of organs, and that every intellectual aptitude, every animal propensity, every aspiration, every sentimental movement, has in the brain its individual instrument. What a helpful auxiliary was here offered to the metaphysician, to the psy-

chologist, to the theologian, to the moralist !
Kant's rare intuition would have caused new
delight in Coleridge, who, by means of this
new potent objective discovery of Gall, could
have given precision, enlargement, definiteness, depth, to the subjective conclusions of
Kant and of himself.

Through the various and urgent activity of
his splendid brain, Coleridge had also given in
to theological speculation. A Unitarian in his
young manhood, he had in middle life plumped
out into a high churchman. But he was too
independent a thinker, and too much of a
thinker, for any body of priests. In her *Introduction* to the *Biographia Literaria*, — an Introduction worthy of her great father, — his
daughter says : " My Father's affectionate respect for Luther is enough to alienate from him
the High Anglican party, and his admiration
of Kant enough to bring him into suspicion
with the anti-philosophic part of the religious
world, — which is the whole of it, except a
very small portion indeed." And here, from
Aids to Reflection, is an aphorism too profoundly true and verifiable to be grateful to
sectarians : " He who begins by loving Christianity better than truth, proceeds by loving

his own sect or church better than Christianity, and ends in loving himself better than all."

Through Spurzheim, a pupil of Gall, who was in London about the year 1826, Coleridge got a glimpse of the great discovery. But whether from being too old (most people are, after forty, to accept a large, new, revolutionary truth), or whether, though having an intellect apt for philosophic search, he yet lacked the warm hospitality to new truths, what may be called the philosophic temperament, which not many even capacious minds are blessed with, or whether he was not just then in the mood for such study, — whatever the cause, while he admitted to his nephew (see *Table Talk*) that "all the coincidences which have been observed could scarcely be by accident," the presentation of the new phenomena did not flash into his mind the light of a new prolific principle, as the fall of an apple did into that of Newton. Had he seized the import of these phenomena, by following the high logic of their revelations, both his philosophy and his theology would have been expanded, clarified.

The division made by Kant of mental faculties under the two heads of *Vernunft* and *Verstand* (Reason and Understanding), — a division which involves the transcendental principles, — he would have discovered to be incomplete and even crude, however firmly grounded in truth, and however admirable as an intuition. On the wings of his fine sensibility, guided now by this new, infallible compass, mounting into the hallowed infinitudes of human spirituality, he would have discovered how deeply and solidly are laid in the constitution of man the saving, elevating principles of hopefulness, justice, love, disinterestedness, and of reverence, "that angel of the world," as Shakespeare calls it.   .

The consciousness of Coleridge, his deep spiritual inwardness, would have made easy for him the acceptance of the commanding position, impregnably fortified by these new phenomena, that, innate in man, are loftiest spiritual and moral capabilities. But as he did not look *into* the phenomena, only *at* them half playfully, the theological fruit of his consciousness remained what it had always been, mere notions, what himself declares the *unica substantia* of Spinosa to be, " a *subject* of the mind and no *object* at all." What lay at the foun-

dation-stone of his theology was not only a subject of the mind, a subjectivity, it was a foreign
fiction, an adopted imagination, for the garden
of Eden and man's fall and consequent expulsion from the garden are Hebrew mythology,
and a mythology which does not imply a very
elevated conception of divine rule and methods.

Modern theology, issuing out of the brains
of mediæval ascetics and scholastic dreamers,
has adopted the fall as its fundamental belief,
all Christian denominations agreeing to make
it the kernel, the soul, of their various creeds.
Being a mere notion, a subject of the mind, a
subject concreted into a fable, an imaginative
representation, it cannot be a perennial source
of binding law, but was from the first doomed
to pass away, and is just now fast losing its
factitious authority. LOVE MERCY, DO JUS-
TICE, WALK HUMBLY, being substantial realities in the depths of man's nature, *objective*
truths, •not mere *subjects* of the mind, being
sovereign principles in Deity and in Humanity,
can never pass away. Astrology is notional,
subjective, Astronomy is objective : theologies
are subjective, transitory, religious and moral
principles are objective, eternal.

Had Coleridge taken the hint offered to him

by a pupil of Gall, a hint almost more pregnant
even than that given to Newton in the fall of
an apple, he would have got to know — not
through his consciousness merely to believe —
that spiritual disinterested impulses are objective principles, inborn in human nature. Belief and truth may be as far asunder as nadir
and zenith. When coincident with truth belief is elevating, when not it is lowering. Belief is often the child of ignorance and egotism,
as is the heathen belief in fetishes and the
Christian belief in relics, and in arbitrary dogmas, which are spiritual relics. Infinitely
easier is it to believe than to know. A faith
may be false, but nothing is so religious as
truth.

Coleridge, with his philosophic faculty, would
have been among the first to acknowledge the
unsoundness of making imaginations the basis
of religious beliefs ; but the " Fall of Man "
and all its theosophic corollaries are so im-
bedded in the modern mind, so interwoven
with the aspirations and spiritual yearnings of
many noble and highly endowed men, that the
dogmatic, mechanical, non-vital elements of
belief usurp upon the dynamic and vital, and
thus lead towards exclusiveness, intolerance,
pharisaism.

But Coleridge was by nature too large and liberal to become the victim of any Calvinistic hardness and narrowess. Through his ecclesiasticism shone the genuine Christian ; and the genuine Christian is he who, convinced of the primordial inherence in man of certain unselfish, spiritual, moral feelings, and of their rightful supremacy in life, aims and strives to make these feelings, and the principles they father, rule in his conduct. He need not, indeed, take cognizance of them theoretically, if he proves that he walks daily in their sunshine, by being just, merciful, hopeful, humble.

Thence it is that the pages of Coleridge have more life and light in them than those of most writers. While he was both a thinker and a poet, he had besides, springing out of his consciousness, a generous conception of the capabilities of human nature. And this conception gives warmth and depth and truth to his delineations and reflections.

From the printed pages of Coleridge, rich, various, and original as they are, we do not get a full image of his mental stature. He had a marvelous, a unique, gift of speech. He was a sovereign talker, sovereign through

the range, elevation, luminousness, fluency of
his talk.   All through his manhood, even from
the days when at Cambridge he drew a choice
circle around him, he instructed, he stimulated,
he awakened men's minds by his affluent,
ready, expressive discourse.   Nay, we have
seen that strangers, visiting Christ's Hospital,
were arrested to listen to the eloquent outgiv-
ings of the charity-boy.

In early manhood Wordsworth, his equal as
poet and thinker, and his senior by two years,
was his pupil, the two friends being to each
other both teacher and scholar.   De Quincey
had the good fortune to come in contact with
Coleridge, or, rather, had the early discern-
ment to seek him, in his own budding manhood, and had his literary and philosophic faculties expanded, encouraged, and emboldened,
his powers all quickened, by converse with one
whose mental gifts he continued through life
to regard with unabated admiration.

But it was in the last quarter of his life,
particularly in its last decade, that Coleridge
was sought for the eloquence and wisdom of
his speech, and that the parlors of Dr. and
Mrs. Gilman at Highgate were resorted to by
many eager, admiring listeners, among them

some of the master-spirits of the age, in whose susceptive brains he sowed ideas that are still coming up laden with nutritious thought. Among these were Arnold of Rugby, who said that Coleridge was the greatest intellect that England had produced within his memory; and Julius Hare, and J. H. Newman, and Maurice, and Hazlitt, who was called a brain-sucker of Coleridge and Carlyle.

Carlyle, in a chapter on Coleridge in the *Life of Sterling*, describes him "as a kind of *Magus*, girt in mystery and enigma; his Dodona oak-grove (Mr. Gilman's house at Highgate) whispering strange things, uncertain whether oracles or jargon." At the same time, almost in the same sentence, he calls Coleridge "A sublime man; who, alone in those dark days, had saved his crown of spiritual manhood, escaping from the black materialisms and revolutionary deluges with 'God, Freedom, Immortality' still his: a King of men.". To one who would have a view of Coleridge in his latter years, when he talked so wonderfully at Highgate, indispensable is this chapter, executed in Carlyle's most vivid strain, at once picturesque and penetrating, broad and keen, touched, though it be, with that grudging jealous spirit toward eminent contemporaries which is a blot on Mr. Carlyle's brilliant page.

Of the soundness of Coleridge's critical and ethical judgments, of his range of knowledge and fertility of resources as exhibited in conversation, we have convincing evidence in the volume of *Table Talk.* And rich as those pages are, they are but a partial expression of what fell from Coleridge in the converse of a dozen years between him and his nephew and son-in-law, Henry Nelson Coleridge. The admiring, but not unduly partial, reporter concludes his preface with these cordial, honest words : "Coleridge himself, — blessings on his gentle memory ! — Coleridge was a frail mortal. He had, indeed, his peculiar weaknesses as well as his unique powers ; sensibilities that an averted look would rack, a heart that would have beaten calmly in the tremblings of an earthquake. He shrank from mere uneasiness like a child, and bore the preparatory agonies of his death-attack like a martyr. Sinned against a thousand times more than sinning, he himself suffered an almost life-long punishment for his errors, whilst the world at large has the unwithering fruit of his labors, his genius, and his sacrifice."

In a thoughtful volume, published ten years ago, entitled *Nouvelles Etudes Morales sur le Temps Présent*, M. Caro, in a paper on Heine, quotes approvingly from the witty German the following passage on Schelling : " Schelling is one of those beings whom nature has endowed with more taste for poetry than poetic faculty, and who, incapable of satisfying the Muses, betake them to the forests of philosophy, where they contract with abstract Hamadriads *liaisons* that are utterly unproductive." A keener stroke of satirical wit it were hard to find ; but that M. Caro is justified in his full approval of it as aimed at Schelling may be doubted, seeing the large place filled by Schelling in the annals of German philosophy. Coleridge, too, had penetrated into the forests of philosophy and got entangled in the "jungle of metaphysics," but, being at the same time a genuine poet, this satire is inapplicable to him.

Philosophy itself, whatever may be the short-comings of philosophers, is a genuine and a great thing, its aim being to reach first principles in all subjects, to get down to and up to primordial elements, controlling causes. He who would master philosophy must descend into the deepest deeps, mount to the highest heights, grasp with his thought the principles which rule all science and all art and all practice. Philosophers, lovers and seekers of this highest wisdom, have failed to compass their object partly from want in themselves of complete mental endowment, partly from want of outward material in the yet imperfectly unfolded human knowledge. Kant was too predominantly intellectual, lacking in full measure the spiritual religious faculties. Coleridge, with a grand intellect, was probably too sentimental, and thence set too much value on ecclesiasticism. Socrates and Plato, whatever may have been their inborn faculty, certainly wanted material, verified data.

That Coleridge had a philosophic mind, that is, a mind that sought and could reach first principles, is apparent in every chapter of his prose volumes. His large discourse of reason, his emotional sensibilities, his sense of the beautiful, give to his pages that unfading life which is sustained by constant reference to the most comprehensive and vital truths.

When, on the 25th of July, 1834, Coleridge passed away from the earth, in his sixty-third year, there was in the minds of the multitude little reverberation of the solemn toll that announced his decease. His name had never been lifted and flattered by the breath of popularity. The funeral bell had a much livelier and wider echo at the decease of Byron or Scott. And yet, the life-work of Coleridge is more valuable than that of either of these. His poetic genius was at least equal to theirs, and he, much more than either of them, dealt in ideas, in generative thought. Only a choice circle felt what a void was made in the intellectual atmosphere of England. The pen and tongue of an original thinker, of an eloquent expounder of fruitful truths, had ceased to move forever.

By one who had known him from boyhood, who for fifty years had enjoyed the privilege of unbroken friendship with him, a touching tribute was paid to Coleridge. For some weeks after his decease, in the midst of conversation among friends, the noble countenance of Charles Lamb would suddenly grow abstracted, and solemnly, half interrogatively, he would exclaim, "Coleridge is dead!" as though such a death were too enormous to be taken into the mind: "Coleridge is dead!"

SHELLEY.

TO SHELLEY.

Upon thy subtile nature was a bloom,
Unearthly in its tender, gleamful glow,
As thou hadst strayed from some sane star where
        blow
But halcyon airs, and here, blinded by gloom,
Didst stumble, for the lack of light and room,
And strike and wound with purposed good ; and
        so,
Through Highest pity, thou hadst leave to go
Early to where for each earth-life its doom
Awaits it, as the fruit the seed, and where
Thy multitudinous imaginings,
So truthful pure, on Heaven's fulgent stair
Fit issue find, and mid the radiant rings
Of mounting Angels thy great spirit's glare
Adds to the brightness of the brightest things.

SHELLEY.

I.

MAN might be symbolized by the attitude of Mercury a-tiptoe on the earth, his figure tending, and his eyes and upper limbs turned, skyward, with wings on his heels, to waft him toward the Heaven whence he came. Man on earth is an aspiring animal, the only animal that aspires, the only animal that can behold the constellations, and, therefore, more than an animal,

" A budded angel graft on clay."

He is both spirit and matter, ethereal and gross, celestial and earthly. The conflict of these within him, — the upward swing of spirit, the downward pull of sense, — while it unfolds and displays his inborn powers, developing and disciplining his nature, schools him for progression and immortality.

The equipment of man being thus compounded of the immeasurable elements of spirit

9

and matter, the scale of humanity is immense, from the black abysms of beastly earthiness in the Emperor Vitellius ascending to the celestial spirituality of Jesus, the lower half of the countless intermediate degrees being represented by Louis Napoleon, who was of the earth earthy, of the world worldly; the upper half by Goethe, in whose orbicular brain there was a prolific equilibrium, and who, being in warm sympathy with all the affections, was yet enough under the supreme sway of the spiritual and moral elements to make *renunciation* his law, and active beneficence his practice, and who, a born poet, became, through his rich humanity, a luminous sage, while he remained a genial man of the world.

High on the upper division of the scale glows Shelley. From spiritual currents were distilled into his brain the finer essences of humanity. His eyes glistened with messages from the Infinite : his was the privilege to hear angels whisper. With the earthy he was not in full sympathy, and from the worldly he was repelled. In him the human compound of spirit and matter lacked closest fusion, and thence his composite being had not the complete elastic play needed for the most effective

outward expression and practical manifestation, such play as is exhibited in the being of
Shakespeare. But Shelley was drowned in
the Mediterranean at the age of thirty. Had
he lived on earth the other twenty-two years,
who can presume to guess what he would or
would not have been or done ?

On the 4th of August, 1792, at Field Place
in Sussex, the seat of his father, Timothy
Shelley, was born PERCY BYSSHE SHELLEY,
whose lot it was, through the light of resplendent poetic genius, to make an ancient and
honorable name forever illustrious. He was
called *Percy* after an aunt distantly connected
with the Northumberland family. Ambition
of aristocratic affiliation must have been inordinate, even desperate, when an aunt's being
"distantly connected" with (not related to)
the house of Northumberland was seized upon
in order to give the infant heir of the Shelleys
the semblance of relationship to the famous
Percys. And see the irony of fate. If by such
spasmodic effort anybody would get a flitting
glimmer of glory, it was not to be the house of
Shelley that this baptismal act would serve,
but the house of Northumberland, thenceforth
presumed to have some kinship to the exalted

poet. To another poet, the greatest of poets, to the transfiguring pen of Shakespeare, this house owes most of its historic renown and all of its immortality. In pertinacity of will, in dauntless courage, Shelley is not unlike his namesake, Shakespeare's great Harry.

The name of Bysshe the poet had from his paternal grandfather, who, born in 1731, was made a baronet in 1806. Bysshe was remarkably handsome, tall, courteous, and clever. He eloped with two heiresses of good family, and thereby strengthened his interest in his county, and at the same time so enlarged his pecuniary basis, that, by economy and shrewd management, he was enabled to leave at his death in 1815 £300,000 in the funds and an estate in land that yielded £20,000 a year. The man who, beginning poor, piled up such a fortune and got himself made a baronet, deserves to be called the refounder of his family. Money and influence got him a title, and the title added to his influence and dignified his wealth.

Sir Bysshe Shelley's eldest son, Timothy, born in 1753, married in 1791 Elizabeth Pilfold, a woman of rare beauty. Of their six children, two sons and four daughters, all

beautiful, the poet was the first-born. Timothy Shelley was a commonplace country gentleman, not cultivated, a little pompous on
occasion, hospitable and kindly, and a good
landlord. One wonders how a mind so unil-
luminated could be the immediate precedent of
a mental blaze. Lightning transpierces dense
material without coruscation; and so the de-
scending stream of genius passes through,
without kindling the brain that is not its destined point of discharge, to explode at the next
human stage in a burst of electric life.

The poet's mother, besides being beautiful,
is said to have been of a mild and liberal nature, intelligent, with some culture. In her
talent for letter-writing she gave token of literary capacity.

More akin was the poet to his grandfather
than to his father. Sir Bysshe had mental
power; he could take the initiative, and he
was independent in his speculative opinions.
His son Timothy he did not like, and would at
times curse him to his face. At the beginning
of the present century the manners of
English gentlemen were coarser than they are
now. Timothy did not go to the trouble of
having speculative opinions; he was a con-

formist and a nominal Christian. Like his
father he swore roundly at times, and like him
was somewhat penurious. As was the case
with most of his class at that day, in morals
his model was Lord Chesterfield, whom he attempted to imitate ; he told his son Percy that
he would provide for any number of illegitimate children, but would not forgive a *mésal-
liance.*

One could linger on the lives of the immediate progenitors of the poet, and delve far
back into genealogy, if the search could yield
any light on the mystery of poetic genius ; but
this celestial fire is as untraceable to its origin
as it is incommunicable when present.

Of Shelley's earliest years nothing is recorded, nor could there be much to record.
To mothers and genuine nurses no two infants
are alike, any more than to shepherds are any
two sheep ; nevertheless, with their little ways
and doings, their tears and smiles, they cannot in their callowness have much individuality, and, like spring buds in an orchard, their
bloom is quickly swallowed up by devouring
sapful growth.

Happily Shelley, as he was in boyhood from
his seventh to his tenth year and later, is

brought before us in the recollections of one of his sisters. A beautiful boy, with large blue eyes, his head covered with ringlets, a slender figure and finely formed hands and feet, he was uncommonly intelligent, gentle, loving, and beloved by every one.

Delight in the marvelous, a hunger to know, interest in the transearthly, showed themselves in these early years, and, backed by his daring spirit, made him a fearless questioner, an ardent investigator. Already the invisible world had great charm for him. As a boy he was haunted by curiosity about death. He longed to see a ghost. He was ever on the watch to catch some glimpse into the mysteries of nature. In that wild, beautiful poem, *Alastor, or the Spirit of Solitude,* written in his early manhood, in an opening passage addressed to the "Mother of this unfathomable world," he says :

" I have made my bed
In charnels and on coffins, where black death
Keeps record of the trophies won from thee,
Hoping to still these obstinate questionings
Of thee and thine, by forcing some lone ghost,
Thy messenger, to render up the tale
Of what we are. In lone and silent hours,
When night makes a weird sound of its own stillness,
Like an inspired and desperate alchymist

Staking his very life on some dark hope,
Have I mixed awful talk and asking looks
With my most innocent love."

At Field Place there was a large garret, and a room which had been closed for years except an entrance made by the removal of a board in the garret floor. This mysterious room Bysshe made the abode of an old alchemist with a long beard. To his sisters, on and about his knees, listening breathless with a " pleasant dread," Bysshe would, evening after evening, weave out of his boy's brain wonderful stories of this magician, promising them that " some day " they should go and see him. Then he would make them enact strange tales, dressing them as spirits and fiends.

A little later, when with premature curiosity he had taken to chemistry, he nearly set fire to the laundry with his experiments. He would collect his sisters and as many other children as he could, place them hand in hand around the nursery-table, and give them a shock with an electric machine. His memory was astonishing ; as a child of eight or nine years he recited Gray's lines on the *Cat and the Goldfish,* after once reading them. At the bidding of his father he would repeat pieces of Latin verse.

His sister relates that he was "full of cheerful fun, and had all the comic vein so agreeable in a household." This is noteworthy; it tends to show what was his essential nature. At home with his sisters and mother, he was cheerful, ready with playful tricks, happy as boys are. At school he came in contact with the coarseness and tyranny of the world, and, being refined, independent, and, though gentle, not acquiescent, contact turned into conflict. An earnest seeker after hidden and forbidden knowledge so early as ten, his mind was in advance of his years. At Sion House, a private academy in Brentford, he kept aloof from boys' games; for him physical sports had no attraction. Already in his brain were fermenting the juices from which were to be distilled some of the most poetically-perfumed pages in our language. The prescribed lessons he mastered without effort. Greek and Latin he seemed to learn by intuition.

Shelley was precocious as boy and as man; he was ahead of his school-fellows, far ahead of his fellow-men. Ever reaching forward for more and better than was around him, instead of sympathy he met with frowning opposition. To one of his nature it was a joy to give pleas-

ure, and he was ever giving offense. The product of his life here turns out to be a source of
delight to all who can value whatever is best in
literature ; but as to himself, he was uncomfortably misplaced. Ever on the stretch after
something purer and higher than he found
about him, he was in boyhood and in youth so
much in conflict with persons and institutions,
that he seemed like one astray on the earth.

Shelley was occasionally subject to somnam-
bulism. This began so early as his tenth year.
Within the sleepwalker are mysterious agen-
cies that move him, that guide him safely along
precipices with his eyes shut, and empower
him to act and speak beside himself, as it were.
For the time a passive instrument, when he
awakes he has no consciousness of what happened in the sleepwalking state.

As boy, as youth, as man, Shelley had a
yearning towards the world of spirits. He
watched and prayed to see a ghost. This was
an unlikeness to his companions that would
help to isolate him. Poets, the higher poets,
are inspired media for the annunciation and
presentation of beauty and truth. Inspiration
descends upon the poet. By mere effort of
will he cannot write a line ; he is dependent

on his Muse. An ideal presentation of the poet were an upturned countenance listening with dreamy, intelligent joy. The poet, the genuine poet, he who is liable to inspiration, is conscious that fresh thoughts, new combinations, flashes of beauty, come to him suddenly, unsought for, unbidden, come, he knows not whence.

Shelley's world was within; but thence he drew inspirations to nourish his aims in the outward world. In these aims there was no self-seeking. At school — and the lesson is repeated at college — boys are taught, with ingenious method, to be selfishly ambitious. The universal system of extreme competition of itself embodies this teaching, and insures its success. Who can make the best show is the best man. And the instruction is bettered at home, most parents being in full accord with the intellectually superior mother who, being asked as to her son at school, whether he was fulfilling her expectations, answered: " Yes : he is ambitious, and that, you know, is everything."

Now Shelley was not ambitious. The aim, the earnest aim, of his manhood and his youth, aye, and of his boyhood, was to better his mind,

to emancipate his fellows. More light in himself and other men, not more power for himself that he might rule other men, this was his
incessant desire. All his pulses throbbed with
love, and therefore he hated tyranny, and he
instinctively felt that ambition is the root of
tyranny. Had ever a noble life so young a
consciousness of its destiny? Did ever a great
man take so early a resolution to be beneficent? Did ever a benefactor leap in boyhood
into his high career? Shelley was about
twelve years of age when he made that lofty
— stern shall I call it? — vow:

> "I will be wise,
> And just, and free, and mild, if in me lies
> Such power."

But the whole passage should be given. Often as it may have been read, it will bear reading again, and should be quoted in full, as it
describes a most important moment in the life
of Shelley:

> "Thoughts of great deeds were mine, dear Friend, when first
> The clouds which wrap this world from youth did pass.
> I do remember well the hour which burst
> My spirit's sleep: a fresh May-dawn it was,
> When I walked forth upon the glittering grass,
> And wept, I knew not why; until there rose,
> From the near school-room, voices, that, alas!

Were but one echo from a world of woes —
The harsh and grating strife of tyrants and of foes.

" And then I clasped my hands and looked around —
But none was near to mock my streaming eyes,
Which poured their wan drops on the sunny ground —
So without shame I spake : ' I will be wise,
And just, and free, and mild, if in me lies
Such power, for I grow weary to behold
The selfish and the strong still tyrannize
Without reproach or check.'   I then controlled
My tears, my heart grew calm, and I was meek and bold.

" And from that hour did I with earnest thought
Heap knowledge from forbidden mines of lore,
Yet nothing that my tyrants knew or taught
I cared to learn, but from that secret store
Wrought linkèd armour for my soul, before
It might walk forth to war among mankind.
Thus power and hope were strengthened more and more
Within me, till there came upon my mind
A sense of loneliness, a thirst with which I pined."

Shelley was always going out of himself.
So deep, and so beautiful in its depths, is human nature, so wonderful in its composite elements and seeming contradictions, that there
is no truth more solid and prolific than this,
that the surest, happiest way of serving one's
self is to forget one's self. Shelley began
when young to practice this profound truth.
As a boy he had the wish to be helpful to

others. When not much more than a child himself he took a sort of paternal interest in children. His sister relates how he wanted to purchase a little girl to bring her up into better conditions. A tumbler, who came to the back door at Field Place to perform her feats, attracted his attention for this purpose. A boy had no means of setting a practical hand to such a project, but his heart was in it. When he went to see his sisters at the boarding-school in Clapham he would ask questions about their comfort. One day his ire was roused at finding one of them with a black mark hung about her neck for some slight offense. His wrath was more against the system than that his sister should be so punished. At the age of fourteen or fifteen his clear pure intuitions told him that for the healthfullest unfolding of the faculties in youthful education more profitable are appeals to the higher feelings than to the lower.

With all this unjuvenile interest in others, this forward-reaching benevolence, Percy was a thorough boy in animal spirits and fondness for fun. On one occasion he came to the school with the elders of the family, and was so full of pranks that the assistance of his cousin Harriet Grove, his first love, had to be invoked to keep the wild boy quiet.

He was fifteen when sent to Eton. At the core of Shelley there was an intense fire that heated his impulses to irresistible momentum, and projected him into manhood prematurely in certain directions. At Eton he was a defiant member of the institution. He defied his teachers by chafing against their rule, and by neglecting their imposed exercises, giving his time to translating Pliny's *Natural History*, and to getting an insight into the mysteries of chemistry and electricity. He defied his school-fellows by standing aloof from their games and sports, by exceptional studies, and more than all by resistance to the fagging system, against which he tried to organize revolt. Fagging, whereby the younger boys were made to do the hests of the older, even at times in menial offices, was the result of aristocratic privilege, which fosters a domineering spirit, combined — strange as this may sound — with a British love of freedom, whose spirit tends by no means to equality, but to each one being free to exercise his powers as he pleases and can. A satirist might say that this combination was soldered together by

English animalism, which is sometimes brutality.

Wanting the bold spirits who take the initiative in resisting tyranny and abuses, civilization would stagnate, its vitality smothered under formalism and usurpation. The most glorious and venerable figures in history are they whose sounder instincts and clearer vision made them beneficent prophets, and whose courageous speech made them martyrs for truth, through the ignorance and obliquity of their contemporaries.

The directors of Eton were too obtuse, and too much ruled by routine in place of principle, to take a hint from the preference of their brightest scholar for natural history, a scholar so bright that without effort he was at the same time one of the foremost in Greek and Latin. The great soul of Shelley revolted against the odious practice of fagging, and by his courage and the individual force of his personality he successfully resisted its application to himself.

His school-fellows would sometimes goad him into a momentary rage, and then run away: their offensive mischievousness he requited by helping them with their tasks. The

boys of his own age are said to have been devoted to him ; but it is the nature and fate of
high gifts to isolate their possessor. That
which is the source of new revealments of
beauty and life, for the delight and profit of
millions through the ages, is often the cause
of unpopularity and even odium among contemporaries. At Eton, Shelley was sometimes
called the "mad Shelley." Genius, having few
fellows, is at first cut off from one of the sweetest joys of humanity, fellow-feeling. This is
the price paid for its superiority. Shelley may
be accounted rarely fortunate in that he found
in one of his teachers a sympathizing friend.
Dr. Lind, a tutor at Eton, appreciated and
loved him, encouraged him in his fondness
for chemistry, and assisted him in the study.
What a boon was this sympathy to his young,
warm, hungering heart, already dimly athrob
with the coming music of *Prometheus* and *Adonais.* The gratitude of Shelley has given Dr.
Lind a twofold immortality, in the form of revered sages, one in the *Revolt of Islam*, the
other in *Prince Athanase,* where he is thus
presented :

"Prince Athanase had one belovèd friend ;
An old, old man, with hair of silver white,

10

And lips where heavenly smiles would hang and blend
  With his wise words, and eyes whose arrowy light
  Shone like the reflex of a thousand minds."

In Shelley "love and life were twins." Love will ever be giving, and in all ways during his whole life Shelley was a giver. When, just before leaving Eton, he received from a publisher forty pounds for *Zastrozzi*, a novel, he spent most of the money in giving a supper to eight of his young friends. *Zastrozzi*, written at the age of seventeen, is described as an extravagant tale, without substance or form. At this early age Shelley dashed courageously into the battle-field of authorship. That he was as crude as he was young, we learn from this, that his favorite poets were Southey and Monk Lewis, and that he delighted in Mrs. Radcliffe's romances. He and his sister Elizabeth offered to Mathews a play of their joint production, which was at once declined. When he was eighteen he sent a poem to Thomas Campbell for his opinion of it. Campbell returned it with the comment that there were only two good lines in it :

  " It seemed as if an angel's sigh
    Had breathed the plaintive symphony."

At this time the beautiful earnest youth

seems to have so magnetized the publisher Stockdale as to make him the instrument of bringing into the world volumes that were, as merchantable wares, of very little value. As Mr. Symonds, in his admirable Life of Shelley, says: "Throughout his life Shelley exercised a wonderful fascination over the people with whom he came in contact, and almost always won his way with them as much by personal charm as by determined and impassioned will."

Between Shelley's quitting Eton and his entering Oxford there is an interval of many months. He is said to have left Eton abruptly, withdrawn to avoid expulsion. This may have been. A youth of seventeen, tender, yearning for love and finding little, disinterested, wrathful at injustice, premature in mental capacity, with the insight and impulsiveness of genius, and with that unreserve which is sometimes an attendant upon genius, wanting in worldly self-restraint and prudence, would, in a public school such as Eton then was, inevitably be a protester and a rebel. But his revolt was the opposite of Lucifer's; it was a revolt, not against God but against the Devil, not against good but against evil. Shel-

ley ever chafed at unjust inequalities. The
world around him — and Eton was a type of
the world — bristled with such inequalities,
was encrusted with the obstructive indurations
of custom, was offensive with soulless formali-
ties and pedantries, with fat pretensions and
lean performance, with lies that would pass
themselves off for truth.

This chapter cannot be more fitly closed
than with a letter from a friend and school-fel-
low of Shelley. Mr. Halliday, one can discern
in his beautiful letter, is a clear-minded, sound-
hearted, genial gentleman, whose name, as
that of one of the few who loved and valued
Shelley, deserves to be associated with that of
the immortal poet.

GLENTHORNE, *February* 27, 1857.

MY DEAR MADAM, — Your letter has taken
me back to the sunny time of boyhood, " when
thought is speech, and speech is truth ;" when
I was the friend and companion of Shelley at
Eton. What brought us together in that small
world was, I suppose, kindred feelings, and
the predominance of fancy and imagination.
Many a long and happy walk have I had with
him in the beautiful neighborhood of dear old

Eton. We used to wander for hours about Clewer, Frogmore, the Park at Windsor, the Terrace; and I was a delighted and willing listener to his marvelous stories of fairy-land, and apparitions, and spirits, and haunted ground; and his speculations were then (for his mind was far more developed than mine) of the world beyond the grave. Another of his favorite rambles was Stoke Park, and the picturesque churchyard, where Gray is said to have written his *Elegy*, of which he was very fond. I was myself far too young to form any estimate of character, but I loved Shelley for his kindliness and affectionate ways: he was not made to endure the rough and boisterous pastime at Eton, and his shy and gentle nature was glad to escape far away to muse over strange fancies, for his mind was reflective, and teeming with deep thought. His lessons were child's play to him, and his power of Latin versification marvelous. I think I remember some long work he had even then commenced, but I never saw it. His love of nature was intense, and the sparkling poetry of his mind shone out of his speaking eye, when he was dwelling on anything good or great. He certainly was not happy at Eton,

for his was a disposition that needed especial
personal superintendence, to watch, and cherish, and direct all his noble aspirations, and
the remarkable tenderness of his heart. He
had great moral courage, and feared nothing
but what was base, and false, and low. He
never joined in the usual sports of the boys,
and, what is remarkable, never went out in a
boat on the river. What I have here set down
will be of little use to you, but will please you
as a sincere, and truthful, and humble tribute
to one whose good name was sadly whispered
away. Shelley said to me, when leaving Oxford under a cloud : " Halliday, I am come to
say good-by to you, if you are not afraid to
be seen with me ! " I saw him once again, in
the autumn of 1814, in London, when he was
glad to introduce me to his wife. I think he
said he was just come from Ireland. You
have done quite right in applying to me direct,
and I am only sorry that I have no anecdotes,
or letters, of that period, to furnish.

I am yours truly,

WALTER S. HALLIDAY.

II

AT the age of eighteen Shelley entered Oxford, an impassioned lover of his cousin, Harriet Grove. A boyish fancy had deepened into ardent devotion. They had corresponded for some time, and looked upon themselves as engaged. About the period that Shelley went to Oxford some startling speculative opinions in one of his letters alarmed Harriet and her parents, and loosened the tie between them, which was entirely severed some months later on his expulsion from college.

Shelley was matriculated as a commoner of University College, Oxford, towards the end of October, 1810. His first appearance is thus described by a fellow-freshman, who happened to sit next to him at the dinner-table in the college hall :

" His figure was slight, and his aspect remarkably youthful, even at our table, where all were very young. He seemed thoughtful and absent. He ate little, and had no acquaintance with any one. I know not how it was that we fell into conversation, for such familiarity was unusual, and, strange to say, much reserve prevailed in a society where there could not possibly be occasion for any. We have often endeavored in vain to recollect in what manner our discourse began, and especially by what transition it passed to a subject sufficiently remote from all the associations we were able to trace. The stranger had expressed an enthusiastic admiration for poetical and imaginative works of the German school. I dissented from his criticisms. He upheld the originality of the German writings. I asserted their want of nature."

They got at once into a warm discussion on the comparative merits of German and Italian literature, talking, as most young and some older men will, earnestly and dogmatically of matters about which they knew little or nothing, as both afterwards confessed to one another. After dinner Shelley's new acquaintance proposed to him that they adjourn to his room. Here Shelley went off with like zeal into a eulogy of the physical sciences, especially chemistry, of which, however, he knew something. His companion gives a picture of him as he appeared on that evening which has the lifelike look of a sun-portrait:

" His features were not symmetrical (the mouth, perhaps, excepted), yet was the effect of the whole extremely powerful. They breathed an animation, a fire, an enthusiasm, a vivid and preternatural intelligence, that I never met with in any other countenance. Nor was the moral expression less beautiful than the intellectual ; for there was a softness, a delicacy, a gentleness, and especially (though this will surprise many) that air of profound religious veneration, that characterizes the best works, and chiefly the frescoes (and into these they infused their whole souls), of the great masters of Florence and of Rome."

He discoursed long about chemistry, sometimes sitting, sometimes standing before the fire, sometimes pacing up and down the room. When the clocks struck seven he said suddenly that he must go to a lecture on mineralogy, from which, he said warmly, he expected great pleasure and instruction. His host's invitation to return to tea he gladly accepted ; then, snatching up his cap, he hurried out of the room, and his footsteps were heard as he ran through the silent quadrangle and along High Street.

In an hour again were heard the footsteps

of one running quickly. Shelley burst into the room, and, shivering while he rubbed his hands over the fire, declared how much he had been disappointed. Few were there and the lecture was dull, languid. "What did the man talk about?" asked the host. "Stones! stones! About stones, stones, stones, nothing but stones! and so dryly. It was wonderfully tiresome."

Stones instead of bread are what even earthiest plodders are liable to receive, especially in youth; but to their buoyant brothers, the idealists, the stones are heavier and harder, and come oftener, even into manhood and age, for, to the last, your idealist hugs the visions of his poetic brain. This dull lecture was but a pebble to some of the stones already thrown at Shelley and to many yet to be thrown. But if they wounded, they never crushed, nor even embittered him. In his soul there was a fervor and force that bore him up, while the idealist found a twofold utterance, in speech and in deeds. His deeds were fragrant with the poetry of disinterestedness, generosity, nobleness, love. His poetry is enriched with the gold of truth and wisdom. The substantiality of Shelley's poetry is not at first apparent, owing to flowers and garlands of blooming imaginations that hang thick about it, just as the countless ribbed lines and delicate tracery mask the solidness of a great cathedral, while they give lightness to its spire and upstretching arches.

The fellow-student with whom Shelley thus became intimate in a day was Thomas Jefferson Hogg, to whose graphic pen we owe, what is a priceless legacy to posterity, a picture of Shelley's short Oxford life, and of his first years afterwards. The two became inseparable friends, talked and read and strolled together, day and night. Hogg was a positivist, who gave in to no imaginative flights, a dry, somewhat caustic humorist. He became in after years an eminent lawyer and staunch tory, but seems to have seized at once the greatness of Shelley.

Among the books they read together was Plato, who is so full of charm and light to those of the thoughtful who are spiritually-minded. To take up with all his soul any theory that struck him favorably was the way with Shelley's earnest, zealous nature. Plato's doctrine of preëxistence delighted him. To children it gave a mysterious significance. One

day, after a long session over Plato, sallying
out for their daily walk, they met on Magda-
len Bridge a woman with a child in her arms.
"Will your baby tell us anything about pre-
existence, madam?" said Shelley, with an earnestness which for a moment alarmed the
mother, who made no reply. Shelley repeated
the question in the same tone, looking wist-
fully at the child. "He cannot speak, sir,"
said the mother serenely. "Worse and worse,"
cried Shelley, with a look of disappointment,
pathetically shaking his long hair about his
beautiful young face. "But surely the babe
can speak if he will, for he is only a few
weeks old; he cannot have forgotten the use
of speech in so short a time." It was a fine
placid boy, who looked up and smiled. Shelley lovingly pressed the fat cheeks with his
fingers, ejaculating, as they walked away,
"How provokingly close are these new-born
babes! But it is not the less certain, notwithstanding the cunning attempts to conceal the
truth, that all knowledge is reminiscence."

In Hogg's account of this Platonic inter-
view with one of the latest comers from ante-
natal realms, there is one omission. He gives
no hint that this was subtle humor. Shelley

was in earnest play with Plato's fanciful theory. Such play is the surest and quickest means of stripping a proposition of its plausibilities, and of showing whether it be a truth or a pretension. Tossing it up into the glancing rays of humor lets in upon it side lights and cross lights that help much to reveal its real nature. Shelley could not have written *Don Quixote*, but earnest as life was to him, he not only had buoyancy to rise mentally above its realities, which he was, indeed, too prone to do, but from this elevation to seize the absurd and gaze at it, not with scorn, but with sympathetic pity. Humor might be defined as a tender, gay efflorescence out of the spiritual faculties. It has a poetic element, but all great poets are not, by virtue of their creative gift, susceptible of humor; witness Dante, Milton, Wordsworth. A very good man may be without humor, but a bad man is inherently incapable of it; his earnestness is a selfish, not a spiritual earnestness. Did Bonaparte ever exhibit a ray of humor? Humor develops itself somewhat late. Shelley gives evidence of it in *Peter Bell the Third*, and in *Swellfoot the Tyrant*.

Shelley's being was founded on love, fed

upon love. His life-blood was quickened by
love, he yearned for love in order to grow, to
put forth his flowers, to ripen his fruit, to outfill his high, beautiful stature. There was no
love at Oxford; instead of love were academic
rules. Here was a warm, a very warm, human being, a most loving and most lovable
young man of eighteen, blooming into manhood, sparkling with intelligence, glowing with
affectionateness. Cold, and bleak, and hard
was everything about, above him. Among
the tutors and professors and head masters
not a soul that cared to gauge the throb of
this great soul. Among the numerous staff
of university officers there was not one who
thought of dismounting from his old spavined
steed of routine to go forward and question
this new recruit. No, indeed, the system was
military in its impersonality.

Here was a chief seat of learning on the
earth, a temple of the Muses, overhung by
the halo of religious consecration. And now
within its walls, just inscribed as a fresh member, was a youth, athirst, beyond his age, for
knowledge, ready, eager to learn, eager to be
taught, outreaching toward the unknown, longing for recognition by invisible power, looking

earnestly for a sign from above. But the signs at Oxford were all from below, a little heavenliness smothered under veils of earthiness, fat places and mechanical performance, in the religion no soul, and thence in the life no daily beauty. When a student at Cambridge Wordsworth became disgusted with the hollowness of his superiors. His biographer and nephew, the Rev. C. Wordsworth, intending to give a playful blow to his uncle's presumption, says : " The youthful undergraduate looked down upon some of his instructors." Bad is it for the pupil when he has a right to look down upon his teachers, but worse for the teachers. Youths, nineteen out of twenty, are willing, are rejoiced, to be taught. Could Shelley, that young visionary Plato, have found a genial Socrates, how he would have loved him, and listened to him, and revered him! We saw what Dr. Lind was to him and he to Dr. Lind. To a fit teacher at Oxford, Shelley would have been docile, pliable, grateful. With what hope he went to the lecture on mineralogy! With what disappointment he came back from it! Hungry for bread, they gave him stones ; eager for principles, for the reason of things, they gave him the dryest facts. And so throughout.

What, for his unfolding and strengthening, the youth entering manhood primarily needs, and the poet especially needs, is sympathy, recognition, appreciation through the heart. His friend Hogg thus eloquently describes the passionate, joyful expectation with which Shelley approached an ancient volume of promise: " His cheeks glowed, his eyes became bright, his whole frame trembled, and his entire attention was immediately swallowed up in the depths of contemplation. The rapid and vigorous conversion of his soul to intellect can only be compared with the instantaneous ignition and combustion, which dazzle the sight, when a bundle of dry reeds, or other light inflammable substance, is thrown upon a fire already rich with accumulated heat."

If, instead of an old volume, there had been a new living man to read ! If among his Oxford teachers a single one had to this glowing uplooking youth put forth a friendly hand, had opened to him a sympathetic heart ! To the poet — and Shelley had in him the material for one of the greatest of poets — the most attractive, the most influential, of created be-

ings is an able, soulful man. The poet's privilege it is to be drawn with resistless force to
the works of God, to outward nature and inward nature, and a soulful man is God's masterpiece.

To a Shelley what was a formal, reserved,
distant tutor or professor ? This youth was
full of sap : he wanted sunshine to help it to
mount, and these people were full of shade and
chill. Years after this period, a gentleman
meeting Shelley at a social party, and seeing
him uncomfortable, remarked that there must
be something wrong about such gatherings
when a man like Shelley was glad to get away
from them. But the social instinct is irrepressible, and ought not to be repressed. People
ought to hold such meetings although a Shelley does not feel comfortable at them. Goethe
has a playful fling at them. A scholar, he relates, having been persuaded to go to such a
party, on being asked afterwards how he liked
the company, answered, "Were they books I
would not read them." But the one social
gathering was not gotten up to please the
scholar, nor the other to give enjoyment to
Shelley; whereas, Oxford was gotten up to
instruct and unfold youth, and here was the

11

brightest of youths, in whom there was more
to unfold than in any other youth at that day
within the confines of the British Isles, and
him Oxford expelled.

Shelley was a diligent reader, an indefatiga-
ble student, but not in the beaten track of college exercises. Besides Plato he read Locke
and Hume, and their followers, the French
materialists. A youth who enjoyed the verse
of Southey and Monk Lewis and delighted in
Mrs. Radcliffe was still young in judgment.
For a time the materialists took him captive.
Like other ardent natures, Shelley concentrated upon what he took in hand all the powers of his mind. He assailed a subject as with
the focused flame of a blowpipe. He poured
the intensest warmth of his faculties upon a
question to make it yield more light. He was
not merely a seeker, but a high-strung seeker,
of knowledge and truth. He wrote letters to
noted people, strangers to him, to open discus-
sions on topics that for the time absorbed him.

In this spirit, under the temporary influence
of Hume, he penned and printed, for private
circulation, two or three pages of reasoning
which he called *The Necessity of Atheism*. This
trifle (for such it was notwithstanding the ter-

rible aspect it wore) a Fellow of another college took to the Head of Shelley's college.
The Head (where was the Heart?) called together his Fellows. They passed a decree ex-
pelling Shelley, engrossed it in due form, and
sealed it with the college seal. They then
summoned Shelley, and asked him if he was
the author of the pamphlet. Upon his refusing to answer : " Then you are expelled," said
the Head Master, "and I desire you to quit the
college early to-morrow morning at the latest."
They handed him the sealed packet, and he
left them. Thus, through the soulless blunder
of one of her colleges, Oxford snatched from
the glittering intellectual diadem that encircles
her venerable brow its brightest jewel, and
trampled it in the mud.

Were these Fellows and their chief Christians? They believed themselves to be, and
on the street and in the halls they passed for
model Christians. O Christ ! in thy holy name
what absurd and what diabolical deeds have
been, and continue to be, enacted. The devil-
self weaves so dark a veil about the soul that
the angel-self is nearly smothered into blind-
ness. How could these Fellows pray to " our
Father which art in Heaven," so unfatherly

and cruel were they to one of God's heaven-liest children! What sense of responsibility had they, except to that cold corporate abstraction, University College? To their pride-stuffed pharisaic ears were inaudible the beat-ings of the warm pulse of an ingenuous, aspiring youth. The Roman satirist's profound words, *maxima debetur puero reverentia*, were shallow paganism to their unchristian hearts. For this beautiful youth, with his angelic coun-tenance, who stood before their judgment-seat they had as much fellow feeling as the scribes around Pilate had for the culprit Jesus. With covetous looks they eyed him as a choice vic-tim. They wanted to show their power, they wanted to show their piety, they wanted to show their academic virtue. And those aca-demic laws, were they made for the young col-legians or the young collegians for them? The executors of those laws, was it designed that their relation to undergraduates should be that of sympathetic protectors, of paternal guard-ians, of kindly helpers? This act looked as though, whatever was their original design, they were become like self-absorbed spiders that greedily spin and stretch their web to catch unwary wanderers.

Here is Hogg's report of Shelley's account of what happened :

"It was a fine spring morning on Lady-day, in the year 1811, when I went to Shelley's rooms ; he was absent ; but before I had collected our books he rushed in. He was terribly agitated. I anxiously inquired what had happened.

"'I am expelled,' he said, as soon as he had recovered himself a little, 'I am expelled! I was sent for suddenly a few minutes ago ; I went to the common room, where I found our master, and two or three of the Fellows. The master produced a copy of the little syllabus, and asked me if I were the author of it. He spoke in a rude, abrupt, and insolent tone. I begged to be informed for what purpose he put the question. No answer was given : but the master loudly and angrily repeated, "Are you the author of this book ? " If I can judge from your manner, I said, you are resolved to punish me, if I should acknowledge that it is my work. If you can prove that it is, produce your evidence ; it is neither just nor lawful to interrogate me in such a case and for such a purpose. Such proceedings would become a court of inquisitors, but not free men in a free

country. " Do you choose to deny that this
is your composition ? " the master reiterated
in the same rude and angry voice.' Shelley
complained much of his violent and ungentle-
manlike deportment, saying, ' I have experi-
enced tyranny and injustice before, and I well
know what vulgar violence is ; but I never met
with such unworthy treatment. I told him
calmly, but firmly, that I was determined not
to answer any questions respecting the publication on the table. He immediately repeated
his demand ; I persisted in my refusal ; and
he said furiously, " Then you are expelled ; and
I desire you will quit the college early to-morrow morning at the latest." One of the Fellows took up two papers, and handed one of
them to me ; here it is.' "

And this young member of University College, who had still three years to grow before
entering legal manhood, against whom, without premonition, was thus suddenly hurled
this thunder-bolt of academic power, what
were his qualities, his inward dispositions?
His daily companion and friend, T. J. Hogg,
describes Shelley as he impressed him at Oxford and afterwards, and his description is confirmed by some of the highest and best men

who knew Shelley during the latter years of his short life. The following are a few of the briefest sentences taken from a number of similar purport found in the pages of Hogg's *Life of Shelley.*

"His speculations were as wild as the experience of twenty-one years has shown them to be ; but the zealous earnestness for the augmentation of knowledge, and the glowing philanthropy and boundless benevolence that marked them, and beamed forth in the whole deportment of that extraordinary boy, are not less astonishing than they would have been if the whole of his glorious anticipations had been prophetic ; for these high qualities, at least, I have never found a parallel."

"In no individual, perhaps, was the moral sense ever more completely developed than in Shelley ; in no being was the perception of right and of wrong more acute."

"As his love of intellectual pursuits was vehement, and the vigor of his genius almost celestial, so were the purity and sanctity of his life most conspicuous."

"I never knew any one so prone to admire as he was, in whom the principle of veneration was so strong."

"I have had the happiness to associate with some of the best specimens of gentlemen ; but with all due deference for those admirable persons (may my candor and my preference be pardoned), I can affirm that Shelley was almost the only example I have yet found that was never wanting, even in the most minute particular, of the infinite and various observances of pure, entire, and perfect gentility."

III.

To the upright, affectionate, sensitive young poet the decree of expulsion from Oxford was a heavy blow. Its first effect was to incense against him his father, who forbade his return to Field Place. It broke off finally his engagement to Harriet Grove; it arrested his studious reading, which the quiet of Oxford favored; it put a brand upon his name in the world. Showered as arrows from the deadly quiver of angered Apollo fell suddenly upon him the shafts of adversity. Did he quail, did he succumb? Can a hurricane blow out the flame of Ætna? The flame bends, writhes before it. As for Shelley, neither his purposes nor his outward being yielded a jot to this concentrated storm. In the depths of his being was a fire too strong and too pure that the flame of his life should even waver before the blast of circumstances. A deep glowing soul kept his gait as upright and steady as itself. Only in his love was he stricken. He loved Harriet Grove. That she should give him up wounded him sorely. Deep compassion, cheered by deeper admiration, holds us as we call up the image of this boy-man, alone in multitudinous London in the summer of 1811, not yet nineteen, with his tall, slight figure and radiant countenance, a refined, courteous, tender gentleman, suddenly bereft of all those outward supports so needful to a youth just passing into manhood, — paternal aid and protection, family sympathy, favor of elders, good-will of friends, — all suddenly snatched from him, and he standing erect, uncrushed, unbowed, undismayed.

By an image so imposing, one's thought is called off from what the name of Shelley brings, before us, his poetry with its inexhaustible imaginations, its aerial flights, its musical reverberations out of the unknown, its sparkling draughts from the fountains of nature, — from all this we are called to gaze with a new admiration at the steadfast manliness, the moral courage, the stoical fortitude, of a youthful figure, wrenched in a moment from its dearest social ties, loosed from all its sweet dependencies.

But to a great soul what are the world's animosities ? They are what to the rising sun

is the darkness of a stormy night. To the
risen sun the darkness has ceased to be. To
the young Shelley, strong and truthful, when
he asserted himself, outward adversities were
not.

Among other hostilities, his father had
stopped his allowance. It is said (and the
statement is readily credible, so in accord is
it with the generous spirit of Shelley's whole
life) that at this time he pawned his solar mi-
croscope, a pet instrument; in order to relieve
a case of distress. In his first disgrace, his
sisters sent him their pocket-money. But the
stoppage of the allowance did not last long.
His father soon relaxed and had him at Field
Place, when an arrangement was made whereby he was allowed two hundred pounds a year.

Shelley's bearing toward his father was not
always what it should have been. In the way
he sometimes spoke to him and of him there
was a want of filial propriety. Through the
Shelleys the paternal stream did not flow clear
and steady ; it was liable to obstructions and
eddies and turbid eruptions. Sir Bysshe, we
have seen, would damn his son Timothy to his
face, and though his son did not repay him in
verbal coin of the same mintage, his affection

and respect could not be expected to maintain
themselves at due filial heat.   Timothy, on his
part, could not understand his son Percy; for
that he should not be blamed.   Many men,
with far more insight and culture than he,
have failed to understand Shelley.   Fully to
appreciate him is needed a healthy, genuinely
Christian sympathy, allied to poetic insight.
The father's obtuseness led to arbitrary or irritating acts.   Percy was certainly as right
not to heed the paternal advice to get himself
converted to the Timothean type of Christianity by reading Paley's *Evidences*, as he was to
disregard the hint in the matter of illegitimate
children.

And now came an event which assuredly
would not have come so soon, nor in the form
it did come in, but for the dislocation of Shelley's life through his expulsion from Oxford,
and the consequent frowns of friends and rela-
tives, the alienation of Harriet Grove, the dis-
satisfaction of his father: I mean his marriage.

Among the schoolmates of his sisters was
Harriet Westbrook, the daughter of a retired London innkeeper.   Harriet was very
pretty, with a slight figure, a sunny countenance, and beautiful hair.   She was the me-

dium through whom his sisters conveyed to
Shelley the savings from their pocket-money.
One day Harriet, accompanied by a much
older sister, came to his lodgings to bring
this little treasure. He had seen Harriet
before. Her name was that of his first love.
She too was lovely, not without accomplishment. Shelley's heart was still warm with
the passion for his cousin. He was a general
lover of women. His ideal of woman was
high, drawn out of his own rich, pure heart.
To him the companionship of woman was a
deep need. To a young poet's imagination
behind beauty lie all other perfections.

Shelley now visited Harriet at her father's
house. Such a visitor had never passed that
threshold before : a young man of rare personal attractions, and heir to a rich baronetcy.
The father and elder sister would not fail to
encourage his visits. Harriet had an illness
which kept her some time at home. Shelley
escorted her back to school. She complained
to him of bad treatment at home. This of itself was enough to blow into a matrimonial
blaze the delicate flame already kindled in
Shelley's heart. He was a man to marry a
lovely woman purely out of pity.

It was for both a misfortune, — the union of these two. They were paired, not mated. Harriet had all the qualities to have suitably filled the place of wife to a commonplace, respectable citizen. For a fervent, aspiring, intellectual poet she was unsuited. Shelley, with his ardor and earnestness, his imaginative discourse, his air and bearing of refined gentlemanhood, his seraphic beauty of countenance, was irresistible to women. Even with Harriet's love for him, their marriage might be called superficial, not molded out of solid sentiment, not grown out of hearty sources. A very pretty, pleasing young woman, whose family worked to bring about a match with a splendidly-gifted young man of great worldly expectations. This is not rightly worded — it should be, a match between a boy and a girl, for at the time of their elopement, about the beginning of September, 1811, Shelley was nineteen, Harriet sixteen. They went straight to Edinburgh, where they were married according to the forms of the Scottish law.

The letters of Shelley to his friend Hogg (who was studying law at York) during the summer of 1811, before the elopement, have great biographical value. They show the in-

gcnuousness and nobility of Shelley, his chival-
rous nature, how easily he could throw him
unselfishly out of himself, and they also show
that Harriet threw herself upon his protection.

Moving about with his bride and her sister
Eliza (who had fastened herself upon them),
Shelley found himself, in the autumn, at Keswick. Here a friendly relation, if not intimacy, grew up between him and Southey. Even
this could not have endured, the two being of
opposite, not to say hostile, types. Southey
looked more to institutions than to the ideas
and principles that underlie them. Shelley
struck right for the heart of a subject, its origin and cause of being. His own soul was
so large and vivid that it ever sought the soul
of things. He did not go too much for principles, — that no one can, — but he did not, even
later, put their due value upon institutions.
In comparison with the mind of Shelley that
of Southey was shallow.

At Oxford, and even earlier, at Eton, Shelley indulged himself in opening epistolary correspondence with any one, though a stranger
to him, whose book or verses pleased him.
Under this impulse he wrote to Felicia Browne,
afterwards Mrs. Hemans, who did not encour-

age the interchange of letters. In this way
he first became acquainted with Leigh Hunt.
He greatly admired Godwin's *Political Justice*, and while at Keswick he began with its
author a correspondence which led to momentous consequences.

When Shelley visited the Lake region he
saw Wordsworth, but Coleridge was absent.
This was unfortunate, and Coleridge himself
regretted it, thinking that he might have been
of service to the young metaphysical poet.
Shelley longed for what he seldom got, —'sympathy. Southey's nature was too shallow and
too unlike that of Shelley to have sympathy
with him, and Wordsworth was not generous
enough to give him much. Coleridge would
have felt with him and for him, and this would
have so affected Shelley that it might have
been a most salutary influence. Like all genuine poets, Shelley cut his own track, but he
was just the man to have received great fur-
therance in the cutting from the brotherly encouragement and the utterances, at once cordial and preëminently intellectual, of so superior a man. Personal intimacy with Coleridge
would have steadied his purposes. Through
direct, kindly intercourse Coleridge would have

won his confidence, as Godwin did through the indirect intercourse of letters.

A distinction of Shelley it is, that more than almost any man of whom we have record, whether philanthropist or martyr, he lived out of himself, serving or striving to serve others. A noble, a celestial distinction is this. The dominant desire of his heart was to help his neighbors, all men. This gives to certain periods of his life a Utopian air. The practical progeny of marriage between a large generous heart and the poetic imagination of an impulsive youth of twenty would not have much bone and muscle.

From Keswick Shelley betook him to Ireland, with the intent of obtaining for the Irish more *political justice* than they had yet enjoyed. He wrote, printed, and circulated an Address to the Irish people. As one means of circulation he threw copies of the Address out of his hotel window. Walking out he would thrust one into the hand of any passer whose visage gave promise of sound political sentiment. One day he convulsed Harriet with laughter by poking one into the hood of a lady. All this was easy to an enthusiastic youth. But had the Address the flightiness and im

12

practicability of a crude, Quixotic brain? Far
from it. Its chief stress was on Catholic emancipation and dissolution of the Legislative
union with England. Catholic emancipation,
after a long struggle, has since been achieved.
Thirty years after Shelley, O'Connell turned a
pretty penny (from six to ten thousand pounds
a year) by ringing the changes on legislative
disunion, and this is now the demand of the
Home Rulers. Shelley also spoke (eloquently,
it was said) at public meetings, once in the
presence of O'Connell and other magnates.
The methods he recommended in his Address
and speeches were peaceful, not violent. In
Shelley there was no bloodthirstiness.

In early spring he recrossed the Irish Channel and took a house at Tanyrallt in Carnar-
vonshire. While there an unusually high tide
broke an embankment, threatening loss and
danger to many cottagers. Shelley took the
matter up with his love-driven vigor, went
about to solicit subscriptions (a hateful duty
to one of his spirit), heading the list with five
hundred pounds. Owing to his promptness
and energy and liberality the embankment
was saved. At this time Shelley's yearly income was four hundred pounds, his father al-

lowing him two hundred pounds, and Harriet's
father the same amount to her.

If on similar occasions every man in a community gave a year's income, the consequences
would be disastrous, and soon there would be
no incomes to give. The watchful activity of
the cumulative impulse is a primary element
of individual, and therefore of general, welfare,
and there is no more likelihood of an overwhelming current setting in against this con-
servative principle than there is that children
playing round their home should with their
little fingers push out its stone foundations.
But, for the higher well-being of communities,
equally indispensable are self-forgetfulness and
self-sacrifice. Gold-capital, important as it is,
is less important than spiritual capital. Without money danger from the breach of the embankment would not have been warded off;
but in the impulse to head the subscription
with five hundred pounds was a spiritual power
that gave life to the whole enterprise. The
giving of such a sum by Shelley was a splendid, an angelic, extravagance. Those who pos-
sess so much spiritual capital that they can
freely commit such extravagances are heavenly lights that illuminate the earth. Among
the courtiers and attendants of Queen Eliza-

beth only Raleigh felt and acted on the impulse
to throw down his cloak. Much greater occasions there are, calling for infinitely deeper
self-sacrifice, when it is immortally becoming
in a man to throw down, not his cloak that a
Queen may step on it dry-shod, but his body
that cottagers may step on it. At rare moments of sympathetic elevation one feels as if
upon one's self weighed the burden of human
misery. You seem responsible for every case
of suffering you meet ; you are ashamed of
your own prosperity. To Shelley such moments were not rare. The feeling of unifica-
tion with all mankind pressed upon him daily.
More than once he arrived at the coach-office
at Great Marlow without money to pay his
fare, having given all he had about him to
poor petitioners on the road between his house
and the office, and thus had to go on foot to
town. He one day entered the grounds of his
neighbor, Mr. Maddocks, without shoes, having just given his to a poor woman.

At the sentence of fine and imprisonment
against John and Leigh Hunt for a libel on
the Prince Regent, "he boiled with indigna-
tion," and offered one hundred pounds towards
the support of the Hunts in prison, and twenty-
five pounds towards paying the fine.

IV.

Society, as an organic institution with spiritual roots, suffers, of course, from violations of its laws. On their observance its well-being depends. In the social organization marriage is a primordial constituent, its inviolability imperative. In the manful upward swing which throughout Christendom has been made in the past fifty years towards larger liberty, much has been thought and said and written about freedom in love. A relaxation of the laws and usages that now predominate over the relations between the sexes would lead, not to more freedom in love, but to more license in lust. Even the most advanced civilized communities could not yet bear any loosening of the marital bonds that have been self-imposed for the common security. The profound Fourier showed his farsightedness nowhere more clearly than when he declared that freedom in love would be the last freedom achieved, and that only when, through the practical application of his great discovery of the law of work

by groups and series, and the consequent lib-
eration of men from most of the oppressions
and abuses and perversions and corruptions
that now afflict and enslave them, only then
would they have become enough purified to be
entitled, and able, to enjoy freedom in love.

In our present social organization this freedom would not be a means to such purification,
but the reverse, and, instead of liberating anybody, would surely lead to a heavier enthrall-
ment and degradation of that sex upon whose
virtue chiefly depends the health and beauty
of the human race, its physical as well as its
moral health and beauty.

Than Shelley no man had a purer love and
higher respect for woman. In him this love
sought a full union, by means of all the faculties, between two beings of different sexes, not
a partial gratification, the full union involving
subjection to the moral and spiritual law, partial gratification involving the demoralizing
breach of that law. But Shelley, from the
very purity of his feelings, as well as from the
impetuosity of his nature, was prone to act out
hastily his desires and conceptions. Amid so
much that is false and foul he was true and
sweet, and so true that he was incorruptible.

He longed to admire, and to be lifted by admiration. His so early enjoyment of Plato showed what depths of good were in him. He sought for men whom he could love and reverence, and he was almost too ready to love and reverence a lovely woman. To a young poet outward loveliness implies inward loveliness.

Harriet Westbrook was lovely to look at, nor have we evidence that she was inwardly unlovely ; but she was made of common opaque clay, while Shelley's clay was luminous with glintings of gold. Between the two there was an inherent fatal unfitness. This unfitness might have been, for some time longer at least, smoothed down by a sense of duty on his part and by pliancy on hers, but for Eliza. Eliza Westbrook was, by a dozen years or more, the elder sister of Harriet, one of those prosaic, persistent, self-sufficient persons, terrible in a household, whose diabolic function it is to deaden the native glow, to stay the streams, of life in those near them, by fearlessly taking upon themselves the direction of other people's vital currents. To her Harriet was still but a child in years, and, from Eliza's autocratic bent, had doubtless always been subordinate to her. Moreover, Eliza had done her part to secure " so brilliant a match " for Harriet, and possibly would exaggerate that part and assume upon the exaggeration. Her presence was thus a misfortune to the young married couple. She was a prickly burr that stuck to them, and, at the same time, a wedge that was daily splitting them further asunder.

To Harriet Shelley dedicated *Queen Mab*, his first long poem, written when he had hardly reached legal manhood. Was the dedication, as well as the poem, in his mind when, nearly ten years later, in 1821, on the occasion of a piratical edition of *Queen Mab*, he wrote this protest : " I doubt not but that it is perfectly worthless in point of literary composition ; and that in all that concerns moral and political speculation, as well as in the subtler discriminations of metaphysical and religious doctrine, it is still more crude and immature. I am a devoted enemy to religious, political, and domestic oppression ; and I regret this publication, not so much from literary vanity as because I fear it is better fitted to injure than to serve the sacred cause of freedom."

If, instead of being rudely expelled from Oxford, Shelley had been treated there with paternal dutifulness, with Christian kindness, it

may be doubted whether *Queen Mab* would
ever have been written. This promising, but
juvenile and crude, performance was probably
a bravado thrown by a defiant athlete into the
teeth of hoary Oxford, — a bravado tempered
by rhythmic verse, but flanked by very out-
spoken prose in the shape of long, elaborate,
heterodox notes, — notes which seventy years
ago, in the then tory-and-bishop-ridden, unfa-
miliar England, looked dark, minatory, danger-
ous, diabolical, damnable. To the present generation, happily more familiar with heretical
freedom and the deeps of thought, far more dis-
enthralled intellectually and spiritually, these
notes wear a very neutral tint, seem threatening only to timid theological laggards, are dan-
gerous to nobody, their diabolism having faded
before that sun of common sense which has
transformed the fearful hoofs and tail of Satan
into materials of fun in comic wood-cuts.

White horses are harder to match than
black : the purer the color, the more apparent
and discordant are the differences when paired.
Poets, from their deeper and warmer sensibilities, which empower them to be spokesmen of
humanity, are harder to mate than other men,
and suffer more from mismating. Of Shelley's

great contemporary peers, one, Keats, died single; only one, Wordsworth, was happily married ; Coleridge lived the last twenty years of his life parted from his wife ; Byron's wife deserted him. The desertion of a husband by his wife has by no means so bad a look as the desertion of a wife by her husband, man, by his resources and position, being better able to take care of himself, and enjoying the honorable privilege of being protector to woman.

Documents are said to exist which relieve Shelley from the burden of blame for quitting Harriet. Probably by mutual agreement they separated. But forty days after parting with Harriet, Shelley, on the 28th of August, 1814, set out from London for Switzerland with Mary. Shelley had somewhat revolutionary theories together with a will and courage to put them into action, — theories which he partly outgrew even before the end of his short life. He was infatuated with the Godwins, he had never loved Harriet with his whole soul, he did so love Mary, who loved him deeply, and was capable of sympathizing with his highest moods, was a pure-minded, high-souled girl, who, as the daughter of Mary Wollstonecraft and William Godwin, felt no need of priestly consecration to sanctify her union with the man she loved. She proved herself a good hearty wife to Shelley, worthy of so great a husband; and he valued and cherished her to the end. Another mismating might have destroyed him. As to Shelley's eccentric proceedings with these two young beauties (Mary was only seventeen), it should be borne in mind that he was young, very young, and that to youth certain indulgences are allowed. Shelley had no carnal wild oats to sow; he was now sowing his spiritual wild oats.

Their bridal tour was as eccentric as their wedding. Unlike similar excursions, it was planned and carried out with severe economy. They started to walk through France, with a mule to carry their luggage, but Shelley having sprained his ankle, they had to provide themselves with a cheap open vehicle. In Switzerland they passed some weeks, and then coming down the Rhine to Cologne in a boat, they returned to England in September, 1814, spending their last guinea to pay the passage from Holland.

It was after this trip that Shelley wrote *Alastor, or the Spirit of Solitude. Alastor*

is the first poem of any length published by
Shelley; for *Queen Mab* was not published,
but only printed for private circulation. *Alastor* shows sure advance in literary skill, being
written in rapid, musical blank verse. Nor
does it attempt to solve problems insoluble by
a young man, or even by ripest age. *Alastor*
is entirely subjective. Shelley delighted in
wandering; he never set up household gods
fixedly anywhere. *Alastor* is a young poet,
"a lovely youth," who early left his "alienated
home" to seek strange truths in undiscovered
lands,

> "Gentle, and brave, and generous, — no lorn bard
> Breathed o'er his dark fate one melodious sigh :
> He lived, he died, he sung, in solitude.
> Strangers have wept to hear his passionate notes,
> And virgins, as unknown he past, have pined
> And wasted for fond love of his wild eyes.
> The fire of those soft orbs has ceased to burn,
> And Silence, too enamored of that voice,
> Locks its mute music in her rugged cell."

He starts on his travel, scattering pearls of
poetry along his path. Shelley makes him
pass through Greece, and Egypt, and Pales-
tine, and Arabia, and Persia, and India; he

> " In joy and exultation held his way ;
> Till in the vale of Cashmire, far within
> Its loneliest dell, where odorous plants entwine

> Beneath the hollow rocks a natural bower,
> Beside a sparkling rivulet he stretched
> His languid limbs. A vision on his sleep
> There came, a dream of hopes that never yet
> Had flushed his cheek. He dreamed a veilèd maid
> Sate near him, talking in low, solemn tones."

To tell dreams is proverbially a bore, and
that the relation of this one is the opposite of
that proves again how in Art everything is in
execution. The sleeping poet has his first love
in a dream, and (the old dream-story) just as
he is about to clasp in his arms the incompara-
ble maiden, she dissolves and the shock wakes
him. All the beautiful sights and sounds of
the visionary scene suddenly non-existent, on
what his waking eyes behold he gazes as va-
cantly

> "As Ocean's moon looks on the moon in Heaven,"

that lovely form forever lost

> " In the wide, pathless desert of dim sleep."

And now, frantic with anguish, driven by
the memory of that dream, he ranges again
through vast spaces, the poet depicting with
poetic vivacity mountain and gorge and river
and lake and forest and cavern. Take this as
a sample of the jewels wherewith the narrative
is brightened ; he is describing the parasites

" starred with ten thousand blossoms," that clasp the gray bark of a double-trunked tree :

> " And, as gamesome infants' eyes,
> With gentle meanings, and most innocent wiles,
> Fold their beams round the hearts of those that love,
> These twine their tendrils with the wedded boughs
> Uniting their close union."

At last, weak and worn, he reaches a green recess where human foot had never pressed. There he lies down, and, faintly smiling, breathes his last. The moral to be drawn from *Alastor* — a moral not then designed by Shelley — is, that it is idle to hope to realize on earth a poet's ideal.

Shelley's passion was for the beautiful, his fervent desire was for the perfect good, his delight was in nature, his rapture in nature's truth and simplicity. He was ever pouring forth admiration, laden with longing for the better, ever " panting for the music which is divine." Hence his lyrical splendor and his lyrical abundance. His brain was an ever heaving ode to beauty and freedom and love. Any event or person or object could become the vent for drawing from this deep, general spring an individual stream of felicitous verse.

Like other of his early poems, and some of

the later, *Alastor* is haunted by the shadow of
death.   One is reminded of that great passage
in the *Phædo* where Socrates declares that we
can only reach that which is the aim of philosophy, namely, wisdom, through death.   Shelley
had a craving to know, to get at the essence of
being.   Truth, wisdom, were wants of his soul.
He had an instinct that death would solve
mysteries that are insoluble on earth.   He read
Plato at Oxford, but before that he longed for
intelligence from the world of spirits, as though
he felt that they could teach him profound
truths.   Those sentences of Socrates would
arrest Shelley more intently than other readers.

When in the winter and spring of 1815 he
was writing *Alastor* he believed that death was
hovering about him, and that his days here below were numbered.   He suffered sharp internal pains.   An eminent London physician pro-
nounced him to be in a rapid consumption.
This was a mistake; in a year or two these
pulmonary symptoms disappeared.   He was,
moreover, pecuniarily embarrassed, and more
than ever isolated.   All this deepened the tone
of melancholy which would be natural to Shelley writing on the *Spirit of Solitude.*   Since

his elopement with Mary the Godwins had ceased to recognize him, and some other friends fell off. But Shelley was a pure great spirit, and therefore not to be bowed by circumstances. No amount of outward pressure could crush or bend that strong soul, with its consciousness of rectitude, its lofty independence, its masterly force of will.

Early in the year 1815 occurred an event which cannot but gladden the pulse of Shelley's biographer, — the decease of a very aged man, grandfather and godfather to the poet. By the death of Sir Bysshe Shelley, his son Timothy succeeded to the estates and title, and Percy Bysshe Shelley became heir-at-law to a rich baronetcy. An arrangement was made whereby the poet received one thousand pounds a year. We venture to surmise that had he been a little more skilled in worldly management, and a little more self-seeking, he could have secured a larger income. Still, an annual sum of one thousand pounds sterling was to a poet in that day comparative wealth. A portion was immediately set apart for Harriet.

Much, no doubt, of his first year's income was preëngaged by incumbrances, some of them incurred to help other people. As to that, however, much of this comfortable provision was preëngaged for every year he lived; for with Shelley life was not life without giving. He lived frugally because it is the part of a sound manly man so to live, and this wisdom enabled him more freely to practice a still higher wisdom, the wisdom of giving. Shelley wanted to keep nothing for himself but the inmost of himself — that, to be sure, was enough to keep.

In the spring of 1816 the Shelleys went again to the Continent, reaching Geneva in May. It happened that a few days after them Lord Byron arrived at the same hotel. Shelley and Byron, who now met for the first time, hired villas not far apart, sailed on the lake together, and became as intimate as two young men could be who were so different, so opposite, in personal and even in poetic qualities, but who each admired the genius of the other.

Goethe said of Byron's *Don Juan*, that it is too empirical, that is, too much drawn from experience; a just criticism which applies to most of what he wrote. In vain did Byron protest, after the publication of the first two cantos of *Childe Harold*, against the inference of the critics that Childe Harold was Byron. But Goethe does not mean merely that Byron drew from personal experience, but that, besides, he depended too much upon all kinds of facts and incidents. There was too much of the actual and not enough ideality. In Beppo, Lara, Conrad, Childe Harold, Don Juan, Byron embodied what was easiest to him, himself. It was difficult for him to get away from the self. Self played too domineering a part in his thoughts and life, and therefore in his poetry, and not a high self. In the creative process Byron had not enough of what might be called spiritual and moral momentum to project him much beyond the personal sphere.

In poetry no poet can create a character except out of his own being ; but that character need not be colored by his own peculiar personality, and it will not be so colored if he has a large elevated nature and prodigal mental resources. Imogen and Falstaff, Iago and Cordelia, came out of Shakespeare's being, but they are not tainted with the individuality and the peculiarities and vices of the daily man, William Shakespeare. In the man Shakespeare there was no virus of egotism so pervasive and irrepressible as to cloud the whole material the poet handles, so that there gets to be a fatally visible likeness among his personages, all running into one another like the differently-colored stripes of a badly dyed tissue. The whole tissue of Byron's poetic characterization is thus discolored and clouded.

A poet's ideals may ascend beyond himself, but, of course, not beyond his capabilities. Sterne did not draw himself in *My Uncle Toby*, nor Cervantes himself in *Don Quixote*, but in these creations they showed their genius for high human ideals, and that their personality was not so egotistically predominant and obtrusive as to frustrate their attempts to embody such ideals. Byron belongs to that numerous class of men, some of them able men, whose egoism withholds them from the culture and happiness and refreshment of admiration. His admirations, such as they were, were by no means directed towards the highest and purest, and his egoism was predominant. Intimacy with Shelley was here of service to him, for Shelley was not only in mind and character superior to any of his previous associates, but he was a living reality superior to any ideal Byron had ever harbored.

If Byron's poetic defect is to fly too near

the earth, too close often to its low places, the
defect of Shelley is too much aptitude to soar
away from the earth to wooded mountain-tops,
and through the clouds towards the stars.   As
the blood in Byron's personages is of a too
dark animal red, that in some of Shelley's
lacks the ruddiness of earthly arteries, being
too transparent with celestial ichor to suit
the best artistic purposes.   His imagery is
at times too unsubstantial for the grasp of ordinary perception.   He delighted to float away
into regions of ever shifting elemental vicissi-
tudes and there launch visionary beings on
their ethereal careers.   Out of his brain he
peopled the air.   Or, is the air, invisible to
grosser senses, alive with sparkling embryos,
which his spiritual eye seized and quickened
into beautiful shapes ?   Shelley is sidereal.
His poetry is a superearthly canopy overhang-
ing us, glittering with the clear, pure twinkle
of stars, and having the beauty and significance of stars, and sometimes their remoteness.
Nevertheless, however distant and aerial is his
range, humanity is ever present to his heart.
In his verse we catch glimpses of a better,
happier future.   For a mind to busy itself lovingly with the future of man is of itself a high

distinction. Deep within Shelley's being lay
a humanity so rich that in following the abundant outflow of his hopes and aspirations one
is swept towards luminous horizons, glowing
vistas as of recovered Paradises. Shelley's imaginations were fed by the divine influences
that unceasingly replenish the pure soul's atmosphere.

V.

THIS summer of 1816 at Geneva was one of •
the happiest and fullest periods of Shelley's
life. Near him, within view, was the sublim-
est of Swiss scenery, which he explored, and
his dwelling was on the shore of the beautiful variegated lake, which he circumnavigated.
And he circumnavigated it with Byron. The
tour in their boat lasted more than a week.

Shelley craved sympathy and congenial
companionship, and seldom got either. This
was the first time that in his companion he
had an equal. The company of Byron was a
delight to him. He probably somewhat over-
rated Byron's performance in poetry. The
difference between Byron's poetry and his
own at first led him to see in it more than
there was. Among Shelley's blessings was
an incapability of envy and jealousy. He admired Byron's verse and enjoyed exchanging
thoughts with him. In their talk together,
Shelley gave more than he received, for his
mind took in principles more readily than By-

ron's, and principles of a higher sweep. Shelley, though now only in his twenty-fourth year, had been already drawn to and had enjoyed Plato. Byron, four years older, could at no age have enjoyed Plato. But he enjoyed Shelley, and after an intimacy of six years, of which this was the beginning, he admired and esteemed him more than any man he had ever known.

The purity and disinterestedness of Shelley's nature made him peculiarly accessible to growth through enjoyment. During these three or four months his splendid faculties ripened rapidly. On the other hand, his impulsiveness and boldness (and the boldness came largely from the purity) projected him into positions where, in a community ruled by custom and inherited law (as all enduring communities must in large measure be), he was much exposed to calamitous repulses. His warm, enthusiastic temper demanded more than the ordinary course of discipline through trouble. A very large share of such discipline fell to him between his fifteenth and his twenty-fifth years.

Shortly after his return to England, in 1816, came the news that Harriet had drowned herself in the Serpentine. From Bath, where they were temporarily staying, he hurried up to London. His agony was intense. This event cast on him a shadow, from the gloom of which he never entirely recovered. It could not but be so. Harriet had loved him, had given herself to him unreservedly. At the first shock of such a blow a man of Shelley's sensibility would blame himself unduly. Afterwards self-reproach would be overshadowed by a darker feeling, as of a mysterious enmity of fate. With all this would mingle tears of pity for poor Harriet. If, a little later, as was reported, he could say of her suicide that it was the act of a "frantic idiot," this was to hide, even from himself, the depth of his anguish.

A few weeks after the death of Harriet, Shelley and Mary were married. They were two years older than when they joined hands. They were of a quality to grow wiser in that lapse of time. They were living in England, not on a far island which they had all to themselves. They had had enough of island life; for the eccentricity of their wedded union had insulated them uncomfortably. A single pair, however pure, cannot contend against the whole married world. To spit against a strong steady wind is to spit in one's own face. That they should decide to live in Rome somewhat as Romans do, was no sacrifice of principle to expediency. Principle has higher tests than self-gratification through pet theories.

Close upon the stunning blow of Harriet's death came another which was the sequent of that. Mr. Westbrook refused to give up to Shelley his and Harriet's two children, and Lord Chancellor Eldon upheld him by a decree which took the children out of Shelley's hands on the ground of opinions in *Queen Mab* and his conduct to Harriet. A stretch of judicial power over individual rights was this, which no tory Lord Chancellor would venture upon to-day. Very hard was it to bear. It wounded Shelley as a parent, it angered him as a citizen; he felt it as a two-fold outrage, — as a wrong and an indignity.

A house at Great Marlow was taken on a long lease by Shelley. There Leigh Hunt visited him, and gives of Shelley's daily life the following account: "He rose early in the morning, walked and read before breakfast, took that meal sparingly, wrote and studied the greater part of the morning, walked and read again, dined on vegetables (for he took neither meat nor wine), conversed with his friends (to whom his house was ever open), again walked out, and usually finished with reading to his wife till ten o'clock, when he went to bed. This was his daily existence. His book was generally Plato, or Homer, or one of the Greek tragedians, or the Bible, in which last he took a great, though peculiar, and often admiring interest. One of his favorite parts was the book of Job."

On Shelley's remarkable *Essay on Christianity* Mr. Symonds makes this sound comment : "We have only to read Shelley's *Essay on Christianity* in order to perceive what reverent admiration he felt for Jesus, and how profoundly he understood the true character of his teaching. That work, brief as it is, forms one of the most valuable extant contributions to a sound theology, and is morally far in advance of the opinions expressed by many who regard themselves as specially qualified to speak on the subject. It is certain that, as Christianity passes beyond its mediæval phase, and casts aside the husk of out-worn dogmas, it will more and more approximate to Shelley's exposition. Here and here only is a vital faith, adapted to the conditions of modern thought, indestructible because essential, and fitted to unite instead of separating minds of divers quality. It may sound paradoxical to claim for Shelley of all men a clear insight into the enduring element of the Christian creed ; but it was precisely his detachment from all its accidents which enabled him to discern its spiritual purity, and placed him in a true relation to its Founder. For those who would neither on the one hand relinquish what is permanent in religion, nor yet on the other deny the inevitable conclusions of modern thought, his teaching is indubitably valuable. His fierce tirades against historic Christianity must be taken as directed against an ecclesiastical system of spiritual tyranny, hypocrisy, and superstition, which in his opinion had retarded the growth of free institutions, and fettered the human intellect. Like Campanella, he distinguished between Christ, who sealed the gospel of charity with his blood, and those Christians who would be the first to crucify their Lord if he returned to earth."

That was a model life for a cultivated country gentleman. But there was in it a feature which made it a shining model for a Christian

gentleman.   He assiduously helped the needy
in Great Marlow ; the sick poor he comforted
at their bedsides.   In London he had walked
the hospitals that he might administer to them.
And his charities were not unconsidered ; he
inquired personally into the circumstances of
those who sought his aid.   At the same time
his house was hospitably open to friends.   Miss
Clairmont and her brother were permanent
guests with him.   At different times he re-
lieved Godwin and Hunt and Peacock with
loans, or rather, with gifts, in two cases gifts
of more than a thousand pounds.

At Great Marlow, in his twenty-fifth year,
working daily for six months, sometimes in his
boat, sometimes on a wooded promontory over-
looking the Thames, Shelley wrote *The Revolt
of Islam.*   Would a painter represent Shelley
in the fervor of poetic activity, he should be
able to put on canvas a young man with a
countenance of singular beauty, intelligence
sparkling through benignity, seated out of
doors, in a boat or under ancient oaks, about
him from the earth a transparent golden haze,
above him a glow of light whence the angels
of purity, freedom, beauty, and truth beam
upon him celestial influence.   Under their

high guardianship and inspiration Shelley ever wrote. In the first period of his brilliant literary career, until his twenty-sixth year, he wrote his longer poems with a distinct moral aim. In the first paragraph of the Preface to *The Revolt of Islam* he avows : " I have sought to enlist the harmony of metrical language, the ethereal combinations of the fancy, the rapid and sudden transitions of human passion, all those elements which essentially compose a poem, in the cause of a liberal and comprehensive morality ; and in the view of kindling within the bosoms of my readers a virtuous enthusiasm for those doctrines of liberty and justice, that faith and hope in something good, which neither violence nor misrepresentation nor prejudice can ever totally extinguish among mankind."

The Revolt of Islam is an historical Epic in twelve Cantos, written in Spenserian stanzas, and making over four thousand five hundred lines. Great though it be as a literary achievement, *The Revolt of Islam* may be looked upon as a preparatory excercitation. Shelley was here straining his poetic bow to test its elastic strength, running the beautiful Spenserian stanza through the whole gamut of its sweetness and its power. He was whetting his finely-tempered weapons, polishing his brilliant armor, practicing his exuberant fancy, strengthening the pinions of his ardent imagination, inflaming its boldness, feeding its power, cultivating its visionariness, steeping it in the moist rainbow of choice diction, girding his young thoughts with young experience. With his hero he might say:

> " With the heart's warfare did I gather food
> To feed my many thoughts, a tameless multitude."

The abundance of thoughts is marvelous, not less so is the poetic buoyancy with which they are winged. There is no want of life, passion, movement, rapidity. But there is a want of density in the materials, and in the handling of them some want of organization. The material is not enough historical and at the same time too much so. The poet wields millions of massed men as though they were single individuals. No human mind can create history; only God can do that. The Poet's counterpart will lack bone; there will be no gritty skeleton behind the flesh, giving to the whole and to each limb firmness, expression.

The hero of this noble poem hopes by elo-

quent words to inspire a whole semi-barbarous
people with the high resolves of his own great
soul, and so to lift them into freedom, — a procedure counter to the possibilities of nature as
man and politics are constituted. Freedom is
a gradual achievement, a very gradual inch by
inch conquest, — an achievement which implies
ages upon ages of persevering, intelligent endeavor, of unquenchable aspiration. Growth,
and slow growth, is a deep beneficent law.
Individual moral freedom is the only stable
foundation for general political freedom. All
human good must be earned, or it will not be
a good. To be sure, in *The Revolt of Islam* the
enterprise fails, and the hero and heroine end
in being martyrs. But the story and the incidents do not take strong hold of the reader's
sympathies. There is not body enough behind the splendid vesture. The whole struct-
ure is too aerial.

Beautiful pictures and scenes, lovely re-
cesses, spirit-stirring sentences, fresh figures
of speech, poetic glimpses, abound. The flow
of high thought, of noble sentiment, is unin-
termitted, and is astonishing by its ease, its
limpidity, its liveliness, its unbroken music, —
music most rhythmical, and so laden with the

breath of wholesome feeling, of manliness, of aspiration, that the reader feels himself, one might almost say, thrilled as by angelic choruses. The twelve Cantos, all palpitating and lustrous with sympathy, with enthusiasm, crowded with felicities of diction, with tuneful reduplications, are a luminous labyrinth, wherein the admiring reader can wander at will with ever freshened delight. Here the imitative, assimilative poet, who has not the originating soul of Shelley, can feather his own poetic nest, while wondering at the countless gems of spontaneous thought, the ceaseless upspringing of new flowers of poetry.

In March, 1818, Shelley, then in his twenty-sixth year, left England for Italy. His health was bad; the seeming pulmonary symptoms were still present. Over Mary and him there came at times a shudder at the thought that the ruthless Lord Chancellor might with rapacious claws pounce upon their two little chicks, as he had upon the other two. (To know how Shelley felt that outrage, read his terrific curse on Lord Eldon, a rhythmic curse of sixteen short stanzas ; also some bitter lines in the *Mask of Anarchy*.) Tyrants and knaves, beware, for your own sakes, how you wound a great poet !

Shelley's income would go much further in
Italy. Generosity and charity kept him always
pinched. Then he longed to be in Italy for
its glorious self, as well as for its milder climate.

Italy told at once favorably upon his health
and spirits. Now began his most richly pro-
ductive period; and such a man's chief joy is
in literary production. In midsummer he went
to Venice to have some more talks with Byron.
Of course Shelley could not approve of Byron's
life at Venice. He was himself unsullied sex-
ually. In his practice he did not break the
healthy wholeness of love, dividing the animal
from the spiritual, — a wholeness upon which
so largely depends the enjoyment, the comfort,
the refinement, the morality, the improvement,
the elevation, of human life. But it was not
for him to be the moral censor of Byron's acts
any more than it was to rebuke his cynical
talk. Of the difference between their views
the reader gets a glimpse in *Julian and Maddalo*, a fruit of this visit.

Julian and Maddalo is one of the most characteristic of Shelley's poems, one of the most
fluent and melodious, and musical fluency is an
eminent excellence of Shelley's verse. Shelley

14

was stimulated by Byron. It is pleasant to think of these two together in a gondola, or galloping on the Lido. Byron never met with a man whose company he enjoyed so much as that of Shelley. It was the highest company he had ever kept, and it is to his honor that he valued so fully the man and the gentleman. Shelley, on his part, felt that he was here appreciated, and by a brother poet, whom he then regarded as greater than himself ; and to be thus appreciated was for him a rare happiness. To both this meeting was a joyous holiday : it raised both to their highest spirits and to their best talk.

How clear an insight Shelley had into the very core of Byron a few lines will show :

> " We descanted, and I (forever still
>   Is it not wise to make the best of ill ?)
>   Argued against despondency, but pride
>   Made my companion take the darker side.
>   The sense that he was greater than his kind
>   Had struck, methinks, his eagle spirit blind
>   By gazing on its own exceeding light."

A little further on, alluding to their talk the evening before, Julian (Shelley) tells Maddalo (Byron) that the words he spoke about man being a passive thing might well have cast "a darkness on my spirit," and then, looking at Byron's little Allegra, he continues :

" See
This lovely child, blithe, innocent, and free,
She spends a happy time with little care,
While we to such sick thoughts subjected are
As came on you last night — it is our will
That thus enchains us to permitted ill —
We might be otherwise — we might be all
We dream of happy, high, majestical.
Where is the love, beauty, and truth we seek
But in our mind ? and if we were not weak
Should we be less in deed than in desire ? "

This is Shelley's noble belief, that in the soul of man there is a divine power, whereby he can cut his way upward towards light and freedom, — a belief which, had he lived, would have vivified and elevated whatever he wrote, and of which his actual work gives beaming intimations. The loaded lines I have italicized tell of the spiritual potency of Shelley's mind. This spirituality, seconded by his keen intelligence, his manly independence, his rare gifts of utterance, made him speak out against the tyrannous abuses which, in the name of religion and of government, have perverted and weighed down the WILL of man. What Shelley now for the first time personally beheld in Italy, the lowering, emasculating, depressive

action, upon the human spirit, of a domineering priesthood, confirmed him in his previous
opinions, — opinions nourished by history and
by sure intuitions.

Bearing on Byron's view of life here is a
striking passage from a lecture on poetry by
that eloquent, large-souled English clergyman,
F. W. Robertson of Brighton :

"Among the former divisions of the egoistic
class of first-rate poets, severe justice compels
me with pain to place Lord Byron. Brought
up under the baleful influences of Calvinism,
which makes sovereign Will the measure of
Right, instead of Right the cause and law of
Will, a system which he all his life hated and
believed, — fancying himself the mark of an
inexorable decree, and bidding a terrible defi-
ance to the unjust One who had fixed his
doom, — no wonder that, as in that strange
phenomenon the spectre of the Brocken, the
traveler sees a gigantic form cast upon the
mists, which he discovers at last to be but his
own shadow ; so, the noble poet went through
life haunted, turn which way he would, with
the gigantic shadow of himself, which obscured
the heavens and turned the light into thick
darkness."

The celestial light Shelley carried within him was ever getting shadowed by earthly clouds. The opinions of Byron and the life he led at Venice, and the life that all Venice was leading, might have darkened the faith of a less spiritually-minded man, but by his in-grown wings of love and rectitude Shelley was empowered to maintain his exaltation above the platitudes and grossnesses about him, holding easily to his belief of a possible better, and keeping his pure ideals ever lively in his soul.

Of the all-transcending might of mind Shelley is a two-fold exemplification, through his rhythmic, splendidly original poetry, and through his tenacity of faith in good and the final triumph of truth. This faith led him back into the dim abysm of Greek mythology to the profound significant fable of Prometheus. Out of chaos Prometheus emerges, lifted by the fire which is to be the means of subduing chaos and of final emancipation from the law of brute force. This fire is a noble, divine soul.

The preface to his *Prometheus* Shelley opens by stating that the Greek tragic poets, in treating mythological and historical subjects, exercised "a certain arbitrary discretion" in the interpretation of a subject. This high precedent he follows; and it may be added, that had he not found the precedent, his moral boldness, inspiring his intellectual force, would have moved him to originate it. Æschylus makes Prometheus purchase reconciliation with Jupiter and his own release by revealing a danger that threatened Jupiter. Here the higher spirituality of Shelley disclosed to him a deeper motive, prompting him not to permit any compromise of principle. This interpretation, while adding to the moral grandeur of the Titan rebel, deepens the æsthetic resources. Shelley makes Prometheus "the type of the highest perfection of moral and intellectual nature, impelled by the purest motives to the best and noblest ends." From the end of the preface I copy the following important passage: "My purpose hitherto has been simply to familiarize the highly refined imagination of the more select classes of poetical readers with beautiful idealisms of moral excellence; aware that, until the mind can love, and admire, and trust, and hope, and endure, reasoned principles of moral conduct are seeds cast upon the highway of life, which the unconscious passenger tramples into dust although they would bear the harvest of his happiness." This passage is more important biographically than critically.

The great Greek mind, adventurous, metaphysical, poetical, insatiable, strove to get down to the root of being, to seize the principles that rule in the creative process, the conditions that prevail in the formation of man, and in his sphere of action. Out of this grew the myth of Prometheus, a poetic effort to embody the conflict, and yet the necessary coöperation, between mind and matter, between substance and form. Around us we daily see this conflict and necessary union between institutions and the needs and principles that produce them. The principles, which are the generative constituent, through the ambitious seeking of those that wield them, are liable to get merged and forgotten in the institutions they have created, and thence to resist change and improvement. Thus they grow oppressive, tyrannizing over those for whose sake was made the incarnation of the spirit in institutions. This is the position and part of Jupiter in the old myth. Prometheus represents the unincarnated spirit that resists the usurpation of Jupiter.

Prometheus being fired by the divine spark
in man that will not submit to passive unpro-
gressive conditions, and Jupiter being possessed by the will that would enforce these
conditions, their quarrel symbolizes the con-
tention between aspiration and stagnancy, —
between free thought and arbitrary coercion,
between the light which leads to high conditions and the darkness that grovels in low.

Brilliant and powerful is the poetic embodiment by Shelley of this high theme.   He gives
full swing to his supreme lyrical genius.   He
calls it *A Lyrical Drama*, but it is the grandest
of lyrics in dramatic form.   The figures, beaming with poetry, are not pulse-thridded bodies,
but shining incarnations of principles and essences in the semblance of bodies.   *Prometheus* himself is not a personage, but the resplendent embodiment of a prolific idea, an
idea by no means ancient, but supremely
modern and spiritual, that man as a soul is
not only indestructible, but, through high will
inspired by love, is creative.   Intellectual
strength, power of resolve and endurance,
lofty aims, are in Shelley's *Prometheus*, but
the might that empowers him finally to triumph over Jupiter is Love.   Love is the re-

deemer of mankind. About the chained martyr gather, to comfort him, from all quarters,
spirits and shapes. Listen to the music one
of these sings to him :

> " On a poet's lips I slept,
> Dreaming like a love-adept
> In the sound his breathing kept.
> Nor seeks nor finds he mortal blisses
> But feeds on the aerial kisses
> Of shapes that haunt thought's wildernesses.
> He will watch from dawn to gloom
> The lake-reflected sun illume
> The yellow bees in the ivy-bloom,
> Nor heed nor see what things they be ;
> But from these create he can
> Forms more real than living man,
> Nurslings of immortality.
> One of these awakened me,
> And I sped to succour thee."

Shelley's brain is an exhaustless spring of
likenesses which his poetic faculty illuminates
into beauty and significance. What freshness
and grandeur there is in this :

> " A howl
> Of cataracts from their thaw-cloven ravines
> Satiates the listening wind, continuous, vast,
> Awful as silence. Hark ! the rushing snow !
> The sun-awakened avalanche ! whose mass,
> Thrice sifted by the storm, had gathered there
> Flake after flake, — in heaven-defying minds
> As thought by thought is piled, till some great truth

> Is loosened, and the nations echo round
> Shaken to their roots, as do the mountains now."

It would not be right to say, that in *Prome-theus* we miss the solidity of Shakespeare, the incorporation of poetry into firm-limbed men and women. *Prometheus* deals in elemental forces, in ideal forms, in voices more than in speakers, in humanized beams of light. One of the Fauns in the second Act asks :

> " Canst thou imagine where those spirits live
> Which make such delicate music in the woods? "

They live in the poet's brain, and so vividly that through his flashing, golden words they are made to live in ours. The choral pages in *Prometheus* are as Shakespearean as the *Puck*-passages in *Midsummer-Night's Dream*, only created with a high, holy purpose. And Prometheus himself is a transfigured Lear, suffer-ing, not for his own willfulness, but suffering through power of soulful will for the emanci-pation of oppressed humanity.

Before *Prometheus* was quite finished, Shel-ley set to work, in May, 1819, upon *The Cenci.* Dante wrote his *Hell* first, long before the *Heaven.* Shelley wrote his Heaven first, and plunged right out of it into Hell, and into the lowest abyss. In Dante's *Hell* there is no pit deep enough and damning enough for Shelley's Francesco Cenci. That a poet, aglow with the love, winged with the splendors, of Shelley's *Prometheus*, should have been able to make himself at home in all the subtlest imaginations of hate and lust and extreme villainy, creating and depicting such a hell as the heart of his Cenci, proves the immense imaginative range of this poet, together with his boundless resources of feeling.

Shakespeare created a Caliban, and Shelley created a Cenci, who is a prosperous Caliban. But is not, in a populous, civilized community, a prosperous Caliban an impossibility? Is it not an extravagant satire, even upon the reeking rottenness of Rome at the end of the sixteenth century, to suppose that one like Shelley's Cenci could have so thriven there, that he could collect around him in his own palace the chief cardinals and princes and dignitaries of the then capital of the world? Cenci is a fiend, a demon, a *blasé* demon, not a man. The lurid glare from his core effaces by its hideousness all poetic light. We cannot even pity him, he is beyond our fellow-feeling, we can hardly wish him redeemed, so far is he below the zero of the human scale in moral deformity. So thickened and darkened by his presence is the whole atmosphere, it is impenetrable to any streak of poetic light. *The Cenci* is a wonderful creation, but is it a poetic tragedy? Is not its all-absorbing chief figure too unhuman for the sympathy that poetic tragedy should awaken? We will not dishonor lions and tigers by calling him a wild beast; they obey natural instincts, he is an unnatural monster; they are terrible, he is horrible.

VI.

THE growth of a great poet, when con
scious of his vocation and his powers, is something to fill the Gods with their sunniest glad-
ness. When, as in the case of Shelley, the
poet is ennobled by the man, earth presents
no more promising, animating process than
such a poet's unfolding. In Italy Shelley's
outward senses were daily cultivated in the
beautiful presence of that chosen land, while
his inward senses, luxuriating at a feast of
memories, were fed by records of the words
and deeds of the lofty men. whose lives have
woven an unfading halo, that draws to Italy,
from generation to generation, many of the
choice spirits of other lands. These, like Shelley and Goethe, climb and revel in a congenial mental atmosphere. The imaginations
of Shelley were here enriched and chastened.
What a crescent fermentation in the brain that
could, within a twelve-month, throw off both
Prometheus and *The Cenci*.

On the partially popular success of *The*

Cenci Mrs. Shelley seized to build a hope that hereby her husband might be moved to make further trials in this new field. Instead of yielding to her persuasions he wrote *The Witch of Atlas*, the most ethereal and fanciful of his poems. The dedication to his wife opens with this stanza:

> "How, my dear Mary, are you critic-bitten
> 　(For vipers kill though dead) by some review, —
> That you condemn these verses I have written,
> 　Because they tell no story false or true?
> What though no mice are caught by a young kitten?
> 　May it not leap or play as grown cats do,
> Till its claws come? Prithee, for this one time,
> 　Content thee with a visionary rhyme."

Conceive of an eagle chained in a close, shady, back-yard, fed on cooked meat from the kitchen; then conceive of him broken loose and soaring through the sunlit air to rejoin his wild mate and eaglets in their mountain eyrie. Like his was the cry of exultation of Shelley when, instead of being constrained to breathe the seething, stifling atmosphere of diabolically perverted passion in *The Cenci*, he found himself careering on unchained imaginations with *The Witch of Atlas*.

But it were a mistake to conclude that, because *The Witch of Atlas* is a "visionary

rhyme," it is outside of humanity, or that because the *Witch* hath the *privilege* of making
the wind, and lightning, and shooting stars her
playmates, and of summoning spirits out of
" the hollow turrets of those high clouds," she
is above sympathy with human beings. She is
exquisitely human ; for, freed from the grossnesses of earthly feeling, a creature woven out
of beauty, she is possessed with love and
cheerfulness, her mission being to show that
all things can profitably intermingle, " through
which the harmony of love can pass." To be
in all ways beautiful, and make the beautiful
sparkle about her glance, like diamonds just
bared to the sun, and to shed wherever she
passes the fragrance of unselfish love, this is
the essence of her being, this is her *raison
d'être.*

In Victor Hugo's brilliant volume on Shakespeare, in one of its most brilliant chapters,
entitled *The Beautiful, the Servant of the Good,*
—a chapter especially dedicated to combating
the tenet *Art for Art's sake,*—there is this very
sound passage : " You say, the Muse is made
to sing, to love, to believe, to pray. I answer
Yes and No. Let us understand one another.
To sing what ? The void. To love what ?

One's self. To believe what? Dogma. To
pray to what? The Idol. No, here is the
truth ; to sing the ideal, to love humanity, to
believe in progress, to pray towards the Infinite." And the following paragraph ends
with these words : " Show me, Genius, thy
foot, and let us see if thou hast, as I have, the
dust of the earth on thy heel."

Now Shelley, fond and capable as he was of
soaring, carried on his heel so much of earth's
dust he always brought some back when he
redescended. However high his flight, never
was broken the cord that bound his heart to
humanity ; and so strong was the beat of that
heart and so warm its blood, that the closer he
comes to his fellows the more musical is the
ring of his verse, the more poetical its tissue.
Thus, when in the latter part of the poem the
Witch

> " Past through the peopled haunts of human kind,
>   Scattering sweet visions from her presence sweet,"

the reader's pulse rises to the intenser throb in
the verse. For example :

> "A pleasure sweet doubtless it was to see
>   Mortals subdued in all the shapes of sleep.
> Here lay two sister twins in infancy ;
>   There, a lone youth who in his dreams did weep ;

Within, two lovers linkèd innocently
  In their loose locks which over both did creep
Like ivy from one stem ; — and there lay calm
Old age with snow-bright hair and folded palm."

Through his exquisite sensibility to the beautiful in its manifold display, in quick alliance with a keen intellect, Shelley was an unsurpassed master of artistic presentation. But for him the most necessary beauty in a poem is moral beauty. As artist Shelley knew the futility of making poems the direct teachers of morals or of anything. The virtue of poetry is in its indirect effect, that is, in awakening higher moods through the beautiful ; and to produce its best effect, it should be vitalized by a moral breath breathed into it unconsciously from the poet's soul. In a letter to Mary in 1818, Shelley writes : "I have been reading the 'Noble Kinsmen,' in which, with the exception of that lovely scene, to which you added so much grace in reading it to me, I have been disappointed. 'The Jailer's Daughter' is a poor imitation, and deformed. The whole story wants moral discrimination and modesty. I do not believe Shakespeare wrote a word of it." From that want of "moral discrimination and modesty" Shelley saga-

15

ciously inferred that this play was not written by Shakespeare. He discerned the spiritual depth there is in Shakespeare, and that to this is largely due his poetic supremacy. The voluminous stream of truth that runs through his plays gets its clearness from its moral fidelity. Hence chiefly it is that in studying Shakespeare we are purified and enlarged. After reading Homer, Michael Angelo felt so exalted that he would examine himself to see whether he was not many feet higher. The profit of poetry is in the expansion, the exaltation, imparted to the reader by the poet, who, through clearer vision, sees and thus depicts objects, events, persons, transfigured, glorified, by the beautiful. As the moral beautiful is the highest beautiful, our expansion, other things being equal, is in proportion to its presence.

Of chastening by tribulation Shelley had more than one man's share. We have seen how troubles thickened about him in his opening manhood. At this moment he was abused, calumniated in journals and reviews, frowned upon by " Society," under a ban in his own family. Peacock, in one of his letters, had expressed a hope to see him soon in England.

Replying to his friend's letter, he writes from Rome in April, 1819: "I believe, my dear P., that you wish us to come back to England. How is it possible? Health, competence, tranquillity,—all these Italy permits and England takes away. I am regarded by all who know or hear of me, except, I think, on the whole, five individuals, as a rare prodigy of crime and pollution, whose look even might infect. Such is the spirit of the English abroad as well as at home."

And he thus scowled upon was the most unselfish, the most generous, the most sympathetic of men, the purest, the truest, the kindest, the bravest, this rare pyramid of excellence being crowned by poetic genius and intellectual splendor. Truly in the first quarter of the present century the upper zone of civilizees was still crude and insusceptible and bigoted and self-sufficient in their ignorance. A fellow-man so supremely god-gifted that he should be a radiance on the earth is invisible to most, and to many who do see him his light is darkness, because not lighted at their feeble, unsavory taper. In the insolence of their blind egoism they would scourge and crucify this divine man, and that chiefly because he does

not go to their church, — and he does not go
to their church because his religion is vital,
of the soul, instead of being formal, of the
tongue.

From the warmth of his yearnings and the
acuteness of his sensibilities, Shelley's troubles
depressed him the more ; but they could not
sour the sweetness of his nature, they could
not harden his heart, — they deepened him.
Turn him into a cynic or a scoffer, or a hater,
they could not, nor drive him to sound the
ocean of human hopes and capabilities with
the broken cord of his own crosses and disappointments.   In Italy, amid the joyful stimulus
of his rare faculties, came two of the heaviest
blows that ever fell upon him.   Mary and he
lost their two children, — Clara, the youngest,
dying at Venice, and William a few months
later at Rome.   For a time they were child-
less, until the 12th of November, 1819, when
another son was born to them at Florence, the
present baronet, Sir Percy Florence Shelley.

To whoever would get a full view of Shelley, his letters, especially those written in his
more mature years from Italy, are an invaluable repository.   Every man's letters are autobiographical, but in the case of Shelley, from

the richness and variety of his mental resources, they are a chapter of biography which
serves to check the most vivid of autobiographical chapters, — that written in his poems, —
and also to rectify or modify impressions made
by the reports of some who were nearest and
dearest to him, — of Hogg, of Trelawney, of
Mary. By no means do his letters make him
appear less lofty in moral stature, less glowing in nature than these devoted, appreciative
friends represent him to be. They bring him
before us even more distinctly than his personal associates do, in his cordiality and unreserve, in his affectionateness and unselfishness ; and they show him heartily interested
in what is going on in the world, ever ready to
lend a helping hand. How refined and self-
forgetful his tone towards Hunt and Peacock
when asking them to do him some small favor
in London, — they who were under such deep
obligations to him, and who seem to have been
worthy of his generosity ; and then his munif-
icence to Godwin. On these precious letters
is stamped the seal of Shelley's high and lovable being, his cordiality, his tenderness, his
sweetness, his disinterestedness, and the unflagging vivacity of his intellect. We come

upon unstudied passages of criticism, upon sentences that give winning insights into himself. In a long letter to Peacock from Ferrara, in 1818, — a letter abounding in genial comments on the people, the agriculture, the climate, the architecture, — after describing the Manuscripts of Tasso and Ariosto, finding in their handwriting an index of their minds, he adds : " You know I always seek in what I see the manifestation of something beyond the present and tangible object." In another letter to the same, a few months later, from Naples, he exclaims : " Oh, if I had health and strength, and equal spirits, what boundless intellectual improvement might I not gather in this wonderful country ! At present I write little else but poetry, and little of that. My first act of *Prometheus* is complete, and I think you would like it. I consider poetry very subordinate to moral and political science, and if I were well, certainly I would aspire to the latter, for I can conceive a great work, embodying the discoveries of all ages, and harmonizing the contending creeds by which mankind have been ruled."

Shelley could not be idle, being in this like all men of full mind. The first need and law of life is motion. The mighty, controlling, creative Spirit works unintermittingly. From this supreme Light Shelley is one of the brightest emanations ever cast upon mankind. When he could not write poetry he betook him to prose. His *Defence of Poetry* is a masterpiece, a broad, eloquent, subtle essay on the greatest of themes. Shelley was ever a zealous servant of the beautiful, the good, the true.

The subjects of his prose essays — thoughtful fragments — are among the most vital and highest that the mind can grasp, — speculations on morals, on metaphysics, on a future state, on the punishment of death, on life, on love, — this last an exquisite, penetrating, spiritual fragment. In the preface to his translation of *The Banquet* one learns how great is his admiration of Plato, and why it is so great. Besides *The Banquet* he translated the *Ion* and passages from *The Republic.* Shelley was among the first to put into English verse several scenes from Goethe's *Faust*, notably the magnificent *Prologue in Heaven*, — a task which would likewise have been poetically congenial to Coleridge, had he not been withheld by what he imagined to be religious reverence. This recalls that rare stroke of wit on dear Coleridge by Swinburne, who says of some of the religious pieces of Coleridge that they leave an unpleasant taste, as of "a rancid unction of piety."

From Homer Shelley translated the long *Hymn to Mercury* of eight hundred lines ; from Euripides the whole of *The Cyclops*, a satyric drama of eight or nine hundred lines ; from Dante several passages ; from Calderon's *Magico Prodigioso* scenes to the amount of seven or eight hundred lines.

When speaking of the mental activity and affluence of Shelley his *Fragments* must not be forgotten.

The entire poetic product of Gray, including translations and Latin poems, does not exceed two thousand lines ; and if were dropped all the lines that owe their beauty to their borrowings, this number would be much reduced. And Gray lived to be fifty-five, and, as he himself informs us, was fond of writing. The number of poems he published during his life was sixteen, making about one thousand lines. Now, the *Fragments* of Shelley, poems begun and unfinished, some of them, like *Charles I.*, *The Triumph of Life*, and *Prince Athanese*, running each to several hundred lines, and many making but one or more stanzas, some of these unpolished torsos, and many waiting for the poet's last touch, — these *Fragments* alone are ninety-seven in number, and cover about four thousand lines, many of these lines loaded with meaning and poetry.

This mass of fragments, shining fragments, is a unique feature in the poetic product of Shelley. None of his contemporaneous peers has it, neither Coleridge, nor Wordsworth, nor Byron, nor Keats. As cause of this something may be attributed to his life being a fragment. It may be believed that had he lived to three score, or even to two score, some of these beginnings would have been carried to their ends, many of the shorter bits would have been worked up; but even then the pile would have remained large, leaving out of account the additions that would surely have been made to it through Shelley's remarkable verbal facility, whereby was seized and secured any fresh thought that darted to the surface from interior depths, or flashed from without, and thus suddenest fancies, abruptest suggestions, were instantly embodied, and, by virtue of poetic demands, rhythmically embodied. Coupled with this facility, which all his rivals, except Wordsworth, shared with him, there was in Shelley an individual eagerness, a fiery precipitance, combined with keenest intellectual vigilance, that pounced upon all poetic prey with the passionateness of the tiger's spring.

One can hardly recall a poet of the first class who did not write profusely. Even Milton, who gave eighteen of his prime years wholly to politics and the cause of civic freedom, left between fifteen and twenty thousand lines. Of course we do not hereby mean to imply that the quantity of verse a poet produces is the measure of his genius, or to hint that, because Shelley, before he was thirty, wrote twenty thousand lines, and Gray, before he was fifty-five, only two thousand, Shelley was ten times as good a poet as Gray. The contrast in quantity is marked only for the purpose of exhibiting the mental prodigality of Shelley, — a prodigality which may be called unparalleled, when is taken into account the high quality of nearly every page that he wrote. Nevertheless, Shelley and Gray do stand in expressive æsthetic contrast to each other, — Gray representing the class of writers who laboriously compose poetry, drawing their material chiefly from without; Shelley representing the class of spontaneous poets, who draw their material chiefly from within, their souls being fresh, deep fountains of thought and poetry.

VII.

SINCE their arrival in Italy Shelley and his wife had moved about, dwelling only for a few months in one place, — at the baths of Lucca, at Este near Venice, at Florence, at Naples, at Rome, leading in each place a secluded life. This continued isolation did not suit Shelley, fond as he was of solitude, and it was oppressive to Mary, who had a healthy liking for social company. In the beginning of 1820 they established themselves at Pisa. Here they had around them a limited but congenial circle. Medwin, a cousin of Shelley, was for a time a guest in their house. With Williams and Jane, his wife, there grew up an intimacy. Shelley and Williams boated together, and to Jane were addressed several sweet poems, among them the one beginning "Ariel to Miranda." Trelawney, manly, clear-headed Trelawney, became a valuable friend to Shelley. Byron, partly to be near Shelley, hired the finest palace in Pisa. The noted Italian surgeon, Vaccá, was an acquaintance. The famous Greek chief, Mavrocordato, visited Shelley and inspired him to write *Hellas*. But the Pisan acquaintance of whom the poet has left the deepest record was a young Italian girl. To her the world owes one of Shelley's most beautiful, most passionate poems, *Epipsychidion*.

Emilia Viviani was shut up in a convent by her father until he should have chosen for her a husband. Shelley, whose noble heart was ever open to sympathy for any form of oppression, was taken to see Emilia, and was fascinated by a loveliness so extraordinary that she seemed to be the realization of even his ideal of feminine beauty. He took Mary to see her. They got permission for her to come to them at times. They sent her flowers and books, for she had more culture than most Italian girls.

In his imaginative ecstasy Emilia became to Shelley the embodiment of that heavenly dream in *Alastor*. Her position as a victim of domestic tyranny heightened to Shelley's eyes the glow of the almost unearthly beauty of Emilia. *Epipsychidion* is the subtlest picture of ideal, uncarnal love. There is pointed significance in the name of the poem : it means *of the soul.* The poem has nothing about the body. In Emilia the poet loves the sudden dazzling revelation of purest poetic imaginings. A creative mind revels and triumphs in the discovery of a preconceived radiance. He calls her "spouse, sister, angel." In the relation between Emilia and Shelley there was not a shadow of evil; nay, there was substantial good, for it gave birth to an immortal poem. As for the "Angel" herself, she was soon taken from the convent to be given to a *sposo* of her father's choice. In a few years she separated from her husband, with her father's approval, and died shortly afterwards, in her real marriage presenting a sad contrast to the ideal union in the Eden-island so wonderfully described in *Epipsychidion:*

> "The wingèd storms, chaunting their thunder-psalm
> To other lands, leave azure chasms of calm
> Over this isle, or weep themselves in dew
> From which its fields and woods ever renew
> Their green and golden immortality."

Although the love of the poet for Emilia was poetical and innocent, and his wife shared his interest in and admiration of her, it is nevertheless not surprising that *Epipsychidion* is the only one of the longer poems of Shelley to which Mary has not written an explanatory note.

To Trelawney the world owes a picture of Shelley in the last year of his life drawn by a masterly hand. A man of rare insight into his fellow-men, Trelawney was at the same time an artist with his pen, an artist the more faithful for his unconsciousness. Both of Shelley and Byron he has left a memorial which is priceless. His own manliness and intelligence captivated both. He became intimate with both, saw them almost daily for several months. One day, a few weeks only after his arrival in Pisa, talking with Shelley of Byron, Shelley cried out to his wife: " Mary, Trelawney has found out Byron already. How stupid we were — how long it took us."

On the 23d of February, 1821, died at Rome, in his twenty-fifth year, John Keats. In the previous autumn, Shelley, hearing of his purposed journey to Italy, had invited Keats to stay with him. In May, 1821, Shelley wrote his great elegy on Keats, *Adonais*.

In another volume (*Brief Essays and Brevities*) I have ventured to call *Adonais* the finest elegy in literature. The subject of *Adonais* is far higher and richer than that of *Lycidas*.

Young King, the subject of Milton's monody, owes his immortality entirely to Milton. Keats is the peer of the immortal Shelley. The mental power of Keats, his wrongs, the resplendent group of poets about him, all these demand a wider range of thought, a deeper movement, more tearful griefs, and these demands are all met with the sweep and glow of intellectual and poetic mastership. In comparison with the heights and deeps of *Adonais*, *Lycidas* is superficial, with an air of elegant conventionality. Every one of the fifty-five Spenserian stanzas, making four hundred and ninety-five lines, quivers with fervor : *Lycidas*, with its one hundred and ninety-three lines is comparatively cold. A curious coincidence it is, that at the time of writing *Lycidas* and *Adonais* Milton and Shelley were each in his twenty-ninth year, while King and Keats were each in his twenty-fifth.

The sustained splendor of *Adonais* is astonishing. Fifty-five Spenserian stanzas, each a new bar of musical thought, each resting, to the eye on, and to the ear supported by, the rhythmic strength of the final Alexandrine; each as fresh and original as a succession of May mornings, every one of which seems to surpass the preceding in the glittering beauty of its auroral dewiness; all glorified by the mysterious creative life out of which spring the earth and the stars. The soul of Shelley was an exhaustless deep of beautiful thought. His imaginations are as poetic as they are abundant. Here is the fourteenth stanza, not more poetical and melodious than others, only, from its subject, more condensed:

> "All he had loved, and moulded into thought,
>   From shape, and hue, and odour, and sweet sound,
>   Lamented Adonais. Morning sought
>   Her eastern watch-tower, and her hair unbound,
>   Wet with the tears which should adorn the ground,
>   Dimmed the aerial eyes that kindle day ;
>   Afar the melancholy thunder moaned,
>   Pale Ocean in unquiet slumber lay,
> And the wild winds flew round, sobbing in their dismay."

The fineness and freshness of Shelley's poetic invention is nowhere more effectively exhibited than where he represents " the quick Dreams " mourning round the body of Keats. No one knew better than Shelley what a gift to the poet — it might be called his capital outfit — is the power of day-dreaming. Take these two stanzas ; they are typical of Shelley, so new, so springy, so laden with musical mind, so inwardly lucent:

IX.

"O, weep for Adonais ! — The quick Dreams,
   The passion-wingèd Ministers of thought,
   Who were his flocks, whom near the living streams
   Of his young spirit he fed, and whom he taught
   The love which was its music, wander not, —
   Wander no more, from kindling brain to brain,
   But droop there, whence they sprung ; and mourn their lot
   Round the cold heart, where, after their sweet pain,
They ne'er will gather strength, or find a home again.

X.

"And one with trembling hands clasps his cold head,
   And fans him with her moonlight wings, and cries :
 'Our love, our hope, our sorrow, is not dead ;
   See, on the silken fringe of his faint eyes,
   Like dew upon a sleeping flower, there lies
   A tear some Dream has loosened from his brain.'
   Lost Angel of a ruined Paradise !
   She knew not 't was her own ; as with no stain
She faded, like a cloud which had outwept its rain."

A poet is great in proportion as out of inward resources he throws light on nature and man, — a new light, because kindled at a new poetic flame. By this recreative illumination man and nature are transfigured, and thence are seen more vividly, because seen more in their reality, that is, in their spiritual being. Hence, the poet's pictures and expositions are true and distinct and beautiful and significant,

not according to the grandeur and variety of
men and scenery his outward eyes have rested
on, but according to the variety and fullness of
his interior wealth of sensibility. A great poet
is a new man, — a new radiant man. Such
is Shelley, and nowhere is his radiance more
new and warming than in *Adonais.* Here are
three more stanzas, ever abloom with poetic
soul. Sixty years ago it was a high, imaginative leap, a prophetic cry, to exclaim, "'T is
Death is dead, not he."

XXXIX.

" Peace, peace ! he is not dead, he doth not sleep —
  He hath awakened from the dream of life —
  'T is we, who, lost in stormy visions, keep
  With phantoms an unprofitable strife,
  And in mad trance, strike with our spirit's knife
  Invulnerable nothings. — *We* decay
  Like corpses in a charnel ; fear and grief
  Convulse us and consume us day by day,
And cold hopes swarm like worms within our living clay.

XL.

" He has outsoared the shadow of our night ;
  Envy and calumny and hate and pain,
  And that unrest which men miscall delight,
  Can touch him not and torture not again ;
  From the contagion of the world's slow stain
  He is secure, and now can never mourn
  A heart grown cold, a head grown gray in vain ;

Nor, when the spirit's self has ceased to burn,
With sparkless ashes load an unlamented urn.

XLI.

" He lives, he wakes — 't is Death is dead, not he ;
    Mourn not for Adonais. — Thou young Dawn
  Turn all thy dew to splendour, for from thee
  The spirit thou lamentest is not gone ;
  Ye caverns and ye forests, cease to moan !
  Cease ye faint flowers and fountains, and thou Air,
  Which like a mourning veil thy scarf hadst thrown
  O'er the abandoned Earth, now leave it bare
Even to the joyous stars which smile on its despair ! "

Whoever has enough poetic susceptibility to
read and study *Adonais* will be able, through
its stanzas, — so alight are they with spiritual
imaginativeness, — better than through almost
any other pages, to get down to the foundations of poetry, to inhale its aromatic essence,
to finger, as it were, its very roots.

Four stanzas of *Adonais* are given by Shelley to himself. Nor are the wonderful stanzas
thus dedicated in the least stained with vanity
or egoism. Appropriate, inevitable, imperative
was it that these few stanzas should be given
to him

" Who in another's fate now wept his own."

That he did so, deepens the pathos of this
great poem. These autobiographical thirty-

six lines are a peerless Elegy on himself by the great poet, a self-portraiture touching and powerful. This is the last of the four stanzas:

XXXIV.

"All stood aloof, and at his partial moan
 Smiled through their tears; well knew that gentle band
 Who in another's fate now wept his own;
 As in the accents of an unknown land,
 He sung new sorrow; sad Urania scanned
The Stranger's mien, and murmured: 'Who art thou?'
 He answered not, but with a sudden hand
Made bare his branded and ensanguined brow,
Which was like Cain's or Christ's — Oh! that it should
    be so!"

It were easy to go on for pages in this strain of eulogy, for each stanza vibrates with feeling embalmed in the fragrance of the beautiful.

The last stanzas are laden with the weird monitions of the seer. Deep sympathy with man makes the thoughtful poet prophetic.

Shelley loved to dally with Death: he was fond of peering over the fence that separates man from the angels. He could not swim. One day, bathing with Trelawney in the Arno, he got into deep water. Trelawney plunged after him and found him lying on the bottom, making no effort to save himself. When he

recovered his breath, he said: "I always find
the bottom of the well, and they say Truth lies
there. In another minute I should have found
it, and you would have found an empty shell.
It is an easy way of getting rid of the body."
Trelawney narrates with great vividness what
on another occasion occurred in a frail little
boat with Jane (Mrs. Williams) and her two
children, when a woman's tact and presence of
mind turned Shelley away from the thought
of "solving the great mystery." The whole
narrative — too long for this page — is strik-
ingly illustrative of Shelley in one of his fearfully inquisitive moods.

In the fifty-second stanza of *Adonais* he exclaims,

> "Die,
> If thou wouldst be with that which thou dost seek !
> Follow where all is fled !"

The next three stanzas conclude the poem:

LIII.

> "Why linger, why turn back, why shrink, my Heart ?
> Thy hopes are gone before : from all things here
> They have departed; thou shouldst now depart !
> A light is past from the revolving year,
> And man, and woman ; and what still is dear
> Attracts to crush, repels to make thee wither.
> The soft sky smiles, — the low wind whispers near ;

' T is Adonais calls ! oh, hasten thither,
No more let Life divide what Death can join together.

LIV.

"That Light whose smile kindles the Universe,
That Beauty in which all things work and move,
That Benediction which the eclipsing Curse
Of birth can quench not, that sustaining Love
Which through the web of being blindly wove
By man and beast and earth and air and sea,
Burns bright or dim, as each are mirrors of
The fire for which all thirst ; now beams on me,
Consuming the last clouds of cold mortality.

LV.

"The breath whose might I have invoked in song
Descends on me ; my spirit's bark is driven,
Far from the shore, far from the trembling throng
Whose sails were never to the tempest given ;
The massy earth and sphered skies are riven !
I am borne darkly, fearfully, afar ;
Whilst burning through the inmost veil of Heaven,
The soul of Adonais, like a star,
Beacons from the abode where the Eternal are."

And now it is time to conclude this *Study*,
so unsatisfactory in its incompleteness, and
yet attractive through its loving fullness of
Shelley. Is he idealized in these insufficient
pages? Who can write faithfully about Shelley without giving into idealization? Happy
if he can reach up to him even then, for he
was an ideality, a great ideal reality. In

studying and getting intimate with Shelley, while one's mind is delightfully exercised, one's idea of humanity is elevated and deepened. He was a man from whose soul sweetest emanations, loftiest aspirings, were as profusely thrown out as are the spring's blossoms that fail not to issue in savory fruit. To build his core the true, the good, the beautiful, were fragrantly interlinked, the bond among them kept ever willing and flexible by the warmth of love.

In *Genevra*, a poem of about two hundred lines, written in 1821, the year before Shelley passed from the earth, there seems to me to be more, than in any other of his works, of what is a characteristic of Shelley, — at once a mark and source of his greatness, — a rich plenitude of mind, pointing to an infinitude of power. Feeling evokes feeling, thought awakens thought, and they leap forth nimbly as if rejoicing to get out of an overcrowded brain. Out of this copiousness are great poems born, such as are many of Shelley's. Among them all, preëminent in pathos, in poetic lightning, in moral might, is *Genevra*.

Were not the ocean so wide and deep, refreshing, fructifying rains would fail us. Only deep, full sensibilities beget poetic deeps, of which, therefore, there are far more in Shelley than in Byron. Byron, talking one day with Shelley and Trelawney, told them that Murray (the publisher) advised him to go back to his " Corsair style to please the ladies." Shelley repelled the advice indignantly, and added : " Write nothing but what your conviction of its truth inspires you to write ; you should give counsel to the wise, not take it from the foolish. Time will reverse the judgment of the vulgar. Contemporary criticism only represents the amount of ignorance genius has to contend with."

Besides *Hellas*, a lyrical drama of thirteen or fourteen hundred lines, Shelley wrote in 1821, including *Adonais* and *Genevra*, about twelve hundred lines in minor poems. All of these, like the poems of all his years, are written from within, — this is the source of their power ; and nearly all were inspired by love, and this gives warmth to their beauty. The *Hymn to Intellectual Beauty* ends with these lines :

> " Thus let thy power, which like the truth
> Of nature on my passive youth
> Descended, to my onward life supply
> Its calm — to one who worships thee,
> And every form containing thee,

Whom, SPIRIT fair, thy spells did bind
To fear himself, and love all human kind."

Between this great *Hymn,* written in his
twenty-fourth year, and *Genevra,* written in his
twenty-ninth, lie inclosed *Mont Blanc, Lines
written among the Euganian Hills, Julian
and Maddalo, Stanzas written in Dejection
near Naples, Ode to the West Wind, The Sensitive Plant, To a Skylark, Ode to Liberty,
Epipsychidion, The Witch of Atlas, Hymn of
Apollo, Ode to Naples, Adonais,* and others
hardly less good, but shorter, besides such
great fragments as *The Triumph of Life* and
Prince Athanese. Add to these *The Cenci* and
his other long poems already noticed, and it
may be asked, Do the poems of any one of
his illustrious contemporaries attain to such
uniformity of excellence? Nay, when are re-
called the five or six best of the above-named
poems, and how in them the finest poetic
essence is breathed through most musically
rhythmic forms, the intense life of fresh substance rounded into blooming gracefulness,
and how, above all, is notable the glowing fusion of all the parts into rapid continuity, —
an especial token this of creative life in the
soul that feeds the flow of lustrous words, —

when all this is before us, may we not ask, not whether Wordsworth or Coleridge or Byron or Keats has surpassed Shelley in the degree of poetic excellence reached, but has any one of them quite equalled him ?

Spontaneity, fervor, sincerity, close clinging together of thought, feeling, and diction, give to each stanza of *Adonais*, of the *Ode to the West Wind*, the *Skylark*, *Hymn of Apollo*, and to every sentence of *Epipsychidion* and of *Genevra*, a buoyancy like that of his own mounting lark,

" As from thy presence showers a rain of melody,"

while the united stanzas or paragraphs of each poem build a whole as compact and surely organized as a swift joyous flight of wild-fowl high up towards heaven, held together in wedge-like symmetry by the invisible cords of divine love kindled in each of them by the creative fire which warms the Universe into oneness, each poem, by this vital concord with consecrated nature, exhibiting a consummation of winged Art.

The richer and deeper the nature the more time is needed for its full earthly unfolding. Shelley, on the day of his drowning, wanted

twenty-seven days to have reached the end of
his thirtieth year. The poetic product of even
Shakespeare, before his thirty-first year, was
not so vast and valuable as that of Shelley,
certainly not so various and matured. Such
maturity may be a sign of rapid development,
as it was with Byron, who at thirty-four had
done his best in poetry. It may be thought
that at thirty Shelley had scaled the summit
of his poetic elevation. But that he was in
the full swing of growth is proved by the
closer tissue, the firmer handling, in *Adonais*,
in *The Cenci*, in *Epipsychidion*, in *Genevra*.
When we consider his temperate habits (he
was a water-drinker and vegetarian), and that
his health was stronger in his latest year than
in several years before; that he was ever aspiring, never vulgarly ambitious; that he was
quickened by a divine sense of the beautiful
which the purity of his nature and his life
kept ever acute; that all this was conspicuous
in his latter verse; that his chief love — he was
a man of many loves — was the love of truth,
truth the resistless leader, the self-renewing
spring of life and new power, — when we consider all this, we can but believe that, had
Shelley lived a score of years longer, his rich,

chaste mind would have gained a more nervous grasp of human life, a tighter hold of the actual, through the warmth of experience, and that many more of his sentences would have become marrowy with that wisdom which is the fruit of marriage between illuminated idealism and heartiest realism.

This was not to be. On the 8th of July, 1822, he and his friend Williams went down in the beautiful Bay of Spezzia, whether by the foundering of their boat in the night-storm, or by her being run into by a felucca, is not certainly ascertained. When Shelley's body was found his hand still clutched a volume of Æschylus, and in his coat pocket was a volume of Keats just lent him by Leigh Hunt, who had arrived at Leghorn a few days before.

In a small band of rare distinction was made a chasm, the width and depth of which the warmest friend of Shelley could not have foreseen, much as he was valued and loved. Retiring, undemonstrative, never self-seeking, he was yet the soul of the circle. His coming was always the awakener of bright expectation, even more on account of the sweetness and unselfishness of his nature and manners, than of the brilliancy of his talk. Byron said of Shelley : "A more perfect gentleman never crossed a drawing-room." When the tall, thin figure of this gentleman, — scholar, poet, thinker, friend, with his mobile, boy-like countenance, his abundant wavy hair, and large blue eyes agleam with the latent lightnings of poetry, a benediction to all mankind behind his expressive features, — whenever he glided in among his friends, his presence was a joyful animation.

When assurance of their loss came home to all hearts there was wild desolation. Leigh Hunt wept and could not be comforted; he felt like a lone one from whose side had just been snatched a whole family of brothers. The pallid countenance of Byron grew paler, and his cynical lips quivered. Even the stout-hearted Trelawney trembled. The suddenly widowed mothers, Mary and Jane, sobbed convulsively in one another's arms, and threw themselves in agony upon their orphan children. Mary was left suddenly in the dark : the light of her life had been quenched. All about her, where there had been bright illumination, was thick gloom. And yet for her, as for every human being in utmost extremity,

there was a possible consolation. When there
should come a lull in the storm of her grief, it
might have been whispered to her :

> Oh, wherefore weep for Percy! he is not dead!
> The thunder-cloud and wind he loved, and sea,
> Have borne his body to its earthen bed
> Of elemental life, while thankful, he
> Springing agaze into the immensity
> Where his creative thought aye joyed to roam,
> His being aglow with livelier life, and free
> From fleshly bonds and bars and fretted foam,
> A raptured angel is he in his heavenly home.

GOETHE.

17

TO GOETHE.

TEUTONIC leader, — in the foremost file
Of that picked corps, whose rapture 't is to feel
With subtler closer sense all woe and weal,
And forge the feeling into rhythmic pile
Of words, so tuned they sing the sigh and smile
Of all humanity, — meek did'st thou kneel
At Nature's pious altars, midst the peal
Of prophet-organs, thy great self the while
All ear and eye, thou greatest of the band,
Whose voices waked their brooding Luther-land, —
At last left lone in Weimar, famed through thee,
Wearing with stately grace thy triple crown
Of science, statesmanship, and poesy,
Enrobed in age and love and rare renown.

GOETHE.[1]

———•———

GERMANY, in her twenty centuries of vigorous life, has been rich in men, many of them men in whom fermented so much of the finer marrow of humanity, that their individual being and doing was the flaming of a light, strong enough to be a new illumination, not to Germany merely, but to Christendom. Of this effulgent class of Germans there is but one man whose life-work exercised, and exercises, a wider and more liberating influence on the thought of the civilized world than John Wolfgang Goethe. That sublime single one is Martin Luther. And the chief glory of Luther is, that he created the conditions, moral and intellectual, that made a Goethe possible.

Goethe was a great poet. This is why we are assembled here to-day to do him honor.

[1] Address delivered before the GOETHE CLUB of the city of New York, January 10, 1877.

A great poet is a great power among men ; he is — what no other great man is, however valued — the personal friend, the intimate, the bosom friend, of every man. In our hearts he makes himself a place, and from that place he warms us, he expands and refines our being: this is his heavenly privilege. And Goethe is much else. Wordsworth is a great poet, so is Shelley, and this is surely enough ; but they are nothing besides. Shakespeare is the greatest of poets ; but from him we have only poems. Save what we can infer from his poetry we know hardly anything of him. These poems, to be sure, are the richest literary bequest ever left to mankind, a legacy which cannot be wasted, a possession which cannot be alienated, through all the ages a grant to every one who chooses to accept it, a gain of light for guidance, an intellectually spiritual gift to every one who will reach out to take it, to the world an inextinguishable illumination, an unceasing beneficence, a force in every soul, a divine presence whose blessing is ever upon us, especially upon us this evening when we are met to talk together of his mighty compeer, second only to him.

Goethe was a chief favorite of fortune. This

form of speech we use because it is not given
to us to delve into mysterious sources and behold the interior workings of the immeasurable, invisible, supervisive power, whose action
is the order and law of our earthly world.
Fortunate was Goethe in the time of his birth,
the very middle of the eighteenth century,
when Europe, agitated as never before by
mental movement, was beginning to heave
with the throes that were soon to burst forth
in fearful revolution. Fortunate in his parents, each a strongly marked individuality ; the
father, devoted to acquirement, — intellectual,
methodical, orderly, precise, a little stern in the
enforcement of rules; the mother, cheerful,
practical, genial, mobile, with the intuitions of
the best womanhood. Fortunate was he in
meeting with the young Duke of Weimar, and
most fortunate in the character and capacity
of the Duke, and equally fortunate in the
character and capacity of the noble Duchess,
Louise of Darmstadt, his consort. But the
chief favoritism was the gift to him of the fire
of genius, which enlivened and made produc-
tive a potent intellect and a rich sensibility.

This union of genius with mental solidity
and versatility, this inward fire warming great

inward resources, would have made Goethe a
distinguished man anywhere at any period.
Still his own principle holds good, that the
Artist, for his unfolding, requires favorable
conditions. A Statesman, a military chief,
is necessarily dependent on outward events;
much more the Artist, who is an Artist partly
through his openness to impressions from without. To be an artist a man must be of more
than common sensibility, of quick impressibil-
ity; he must be one who, through the poetic,
the supreme gift, projects out of himself, in
forms of beauty, conceptions and visions, the
material for these forms being supplied by a
keen perception of and warm susceptibility to
what is present, what is around him, what is
before his senses. The young Goethe, palpitating with this susceptibility, was a many-
sided mirror in the midst of an insurrection-
ary world, a beautifying mirror, on which
struck, to be poetically reflected, its scenes
and passions. His was a large soul, yearning
in its depths with all the mysterious feeling of
a prolific epoch, — a fresh clear mind, a vast
mind, passionate, reflective, creative, with the
power, and the unconscious impulse, to give
voice to the wants and feelings of an impassioned age.

Time and place were propitious; and so, in Goethe's twenty-third year, Goetz von Berlichingen burst into life, Goetz with the iron hand, a protesting shout against the tyranny of custom, a defiant assertion of individual independence, a revolutionary shock to literature, a tearing up of worn dramatic highways, a startling new phenomenon. Right upon Goetz came Werther, which may be called a musical shriek of despair, a shriek that sent a thrill through the heart of Germany, of Europe. Suddenly, with two bounds, the young giant leapt into a great renown.

This renown brought him into contact with Karl August, Duke of Weimar. Goethe was twenty-six when he went to Weimar. On the invitation of the Duke he came to spend a few weeks : he staid fifty-seven years. He began by leading the gay, wild court life of fun and frolic, led by a young sovereign full of force and animal spirits, and not yet out of his teens : he remained to teach the Duke how to work and how to govern. He began, the centre of an admiring circle of waltzers : he ended by being the head of a band of workers, scientific, artistic, political workers, who wrought the Duchy of Weimar into the brighest domain of

Germany. He came as a temporary, spark-·
ling guest : he remained as a permanent, solid
benefactor.

The opening season, the first decade, of
Goethe's living and doing in Weimar presents
a unique picture of what a young man can
perform, — a performance, in this case, which
if not so imposing as that of the young Napoleon in the first ten adult years of his wonderful career, is more spiritually instructive as an
example, and more valuable in its practical
bearings. The Duke, fascinated by the talk
and demeanor of him whom Wieland called
" the godlike splendid youth," as others were
fascinated, as Wieland himself was, and the
dowager-Duchess and Duchess Louise, and all
the Court, the Duke soon began to feel the
deeper attraction of Goethe's mind and character, and to perceive how useful Goethe
might be to him, — a perception sharpened, if
not originated, by growing attachment to his
young friend, who, so young, was seven years
older than himself. Karl August was a pro-
gressive man, one not afraid of new ideas, new
discoveries, new principles. Men of aspiration
and of culture, and of confident readiness to
grasp fresh thought and to recognize its ex-

pansive potency, such men are stamped by nature with superiority; they are the élite among their fellows.

The Duke and Goethe began by playing together: very soon they took to working together, and the Duke, with that rare insight and judgment which quickly discern and appreciate greatness, and which are the most legitimate titles to sovereignty, raised Goethe, six months after his arrival, to a seat in the Privy Council, with corresponding title and salary. Goethe was twenty-seven, Karl August twenty.

With a deep groan groaned the official world, and red tape turned pale. A young, unknown stranger, and a plebeian, without drudging through the subordinate grades, lifted suddenly over the heads of faithful old servants of routine! All Weimar howled! So bristling was the discontent it took the form of a written protest from the Duke's ministers. The boy-Duke held firm. He was a genuine Duke, a leader. He felt that by his side he had a man worth more than scores of ordinary privy councillors and ministers. In this young stranger he had got possession of a powerful genius, that is, a man whose brain is full of

light. And soon — as is the way with a powerful genius, when furthered and not obstructed
— Goethe began to penetrate, to guide all departments.

Among his superiorities Goethe had the
organizing capacity, and to make things better was a need of his nature. He improved
the public-school system of the Duchy ; he
put new life into the University of Jena ; he
brought order into the finances, and made the
generous Duke a wiser economist. He re-
opened the neglected mines of Ilmenau, having
taken hold of Science, — for which he had a
natural aptitude, — in order that he might do
more thorough service in several administra-
tive departments ; he established a fire-brigade ;
in the middle of the night he would leap out
of bed at a cry of fire, and hurry to a neighboring village, coming back in the morning with
feet blistered and hair singed. He rode from
town to town to superintend the drafting of
men for the war contingent ; with the master
of the forests he would ride through the public
domain, teaching and learning. He reformed
and directed the theatre, and created the beautiful park at Weimar. When the President of
the Chambers died, the Duke insisted that he

should fill that place too. He was the soul of the government, the good genius of the community, throwing the light of a piercing intelligence upon all public interests, seeing to everything, teaching everybody, helping everybody, uplifting everybody : the most efficient of practical workers, openly beneficent, secretly charitable. The case related by Lewes, in his admirable Life of Goethe, of his having upheld and supported for years, by sympathy and money, a desolate man whom he had never seen, is one of the most touching and beautiful exemplifications ever brought to light of the refined and generous spirit of the Christian gentleman. During this early period Merk, the cynic, wrote from Weimar : " Who can withstand the disinterestedness of this man ? " It was Goethe's happiness to lend a helping hand to artists and other men of worth. He induced the Duke to call Herder to Weimar as court-chaplain. His influence it was that had Schiller appointed to a professorship in Jena, and afterwards obtained a pension for him, which enabled Schiller to domesticate himself in Weimar. He helped to get some of Wieland's numerous children provided for.

In the midst of this various work, as the

chief steward of the Duke and Duchy, Goethe found time, nay, he gave his best time, his brightest moments, to poetry, working at *Faust*, or *Wilhelm Meister*, or *Iphigenia*, according to the mood, or throwing off some of those matchless lyrics that bloom perennially in their simplicity and significance, ever as fresh and fragrant as the newest, sweetest flowers of a June morning.

When one takes into view what Goethe wrought in those first ten years of his young manhood, how he shone in all places upon all men, how he grew so deeply into the thoughts of men that while he was in Italy Weimar suffered as in eclipse, her sunlight withdrawn from her, we can, without much extravagance, figure him to ourselves, in his beaming creativeness and magnetic beauty, as akin to the Apollo of Greek imagination, a very God of poetry, honored too as the healer, and the harmonizer of discords.

And now, at the end of ten such well-worked years, he had earned a holiday. In the beginning of the autumn of 1786, his purpose made known to no one but the Duke, he slipped away, and under an assumed name, — that he might not be obstructed by his re-

nown, — crossing the Alps, he found himself
in Italy. His feeling towards Italy had come
to be a yearning.

In one of those original sagacious sentences
that abound in him Goethe says, you cannot
enter a room where hangs an engraving and
go out the same as you came in. Active in
him was the liability to be transformed by impressions from without ; and this liability is a
primary qualification of the poet, for it comes
from the warmth and readiness of the man's
feelings. The image of an object without,
falling upon rich emotional capabilities within,
a flame is enkindled which, purified by sensibility to the beautiful, is the very substance of
poetry. During the eighteen months that
Goethe passed in Italy his susceptive, hungry
mind was in a glow. Of this light he made
the most, working in his best moments, at
Rome and Naples, at unfinished manuscripts
he had brought with him. From Italy he
came back refreshed, strengthened, calmed ;
his horizon enlarged, his appetite for knowledge allayed, his thoughts on Art harmonized,
compacted. He returned, not to resume his
former manifold functions, but to dedicate himself to his inborn vocation, poetry and litera-

ture, retaining control only over the artistic
and scientific institutions of Weimar. Upon
them he brought to bear his vast acquired
knowledge, his ripened thoughtfulness, and
while serving them, through such service
deepening, refining his own culture.

Goethe was an incessant worker, an unceasing learner. Simply by supplying the needs
of his own nature, his life was the putting in
practice of a broad counsel of Voltaire: " Give
to the soul all possible forms : it is a fire which
God has confided to us : we should feed it with
whatever is most precious. Our being should
be made to partake of all imaginable conditions : the doors of the mind should be opened
to all knowledge, all feeling. Provided they
don't enter pell-mell, there is room for all."
And this counsel Goethe could follow, because,
having an omnivorous appetite for whatever
can be known and whatever can be felt, he had
within his intellect that high logical method —
an indispensable requirement for all large performance — which could so class and coördinate his vast stores as to have them all readily
available, and make room for an endless supply. No man ever held closer, wiser watch
over his knowledge and his feelings, in order

to keep his stores sweet and incorruptible. In all efforts, practical and theoretical, for founding or bettering institutions, for combating or diffusing ideas, he strove to obey — and for obeying had clearer insights, deeper intuitions, than most men — the mandate conveyed in the simple words of Jesus : " Every plant which my Heavenly Father has not planted shall be rooted up." Seeking always, unremittingly, through four score years, his personal improvement, — improvement moral, æsthetical, intellectual, — intently did he aim to make these profound words the touchstone of his own inward motions.

After middle life Goethe wrote: "I, who have known and suffered from the perpetual agitation of feelings and opinions in myself and in others, delight in the sublime repose which is produced by contact with the great and eloquent silence of nature." The man who " suffers from the perpetual agitation of feelings in himself and others " is endowed with richest material for poetry : he suffers because he feels so keenly. Sympathy is the poet's capital ; and when to this wealth of sensibility he adds the decisive poetic gift, sense of the beautiful, the refining transfigur-

ing power, he is a poet *in posse*, for he pos-
sesses "the vision and the faculty divine."
To be a poet *in esse*, he must have in further addition the "accomplishment of verse."
Wordsworth says:

> "Oh, many are the poets that are sown
> By nature; men endowed with highest gifts,
> The vision and the faculty divine,
> Yet wanting the accomplishment of verse."

So, too, with poetic painters: some, with
fine gifts, cannot acquire manipulating dexter-
ity. This seems to have been the case with
Hazlitt, and somewhat with Haydon, who
thence failed as Artists; for it is the power
adequately to embody poetic conceptions and
feelings that makes the Artist. When Coleridge says of Shakespeare that his judgment
is equal to his genius, he proclaims him a
great Artist. Shakespeare's intellectual resources for turning to best account his deep
glowing sensibilities were of the highest. To
his great conceptions he knew how to give
dramatic form with a nicety of adaptation,
with an accuracy of adjustment, which show
them to the best advantage. He has the art
to incarnate his ideas and feelings in firm,
brilliant, transparent forms, and he has a sure
eye for proportion.

Never did man more fully than Goethe earn the high title of Artist. I call it a high title, because genuine Art, really Fine Art, implies the power of giving expression to poetic thought and sentiment, and, in its highest range, to broadest and deepest poetic thought and sentiment. There can be no Fine Art without "the vision and the faculty divine." Facility in clothing thought with words, rare definiteness of perception, delight in the concrete, — the combination of aptitudes that empower the poetic mind to give clean, clear expression to its workings, and with these the instinct and judgment to choose the most fitting form, — in all this Goethe is unsurpassed. Thence in his performance there is the grace and buoyancy which are the charm of the best Art.

From his brief epigrams and distichs to songs and ballads, and thence to his longer poems, *Iphigenia*, and *Tasso*, and *Herman, and Dorothea*, and *Faust*, in all there is, I had almost said, artistic perfection, resulting from the harmonious marriage between sentiment and diction, between thought and word, between substance and form. His best work — and much of it is best — is truly classical;

that is, it embodies healthy sentiment, just thought, in choice language the most fitting to express them. A high characteristic of Goethe is his simplicity of diction, — a quality by no means common to all good poets, — which in him comes from the clearness of his mind and his sincerity. All Goethe's works are the offspring of his interior self. His pen took no bribes from vanity or ambition, or from poverty. Especially were his works the offspring of his love. What he wrote he wrote from sympathy with his subject, — the only pure source of literary work; and how wide were his sympathies may be learned from the unprecedented range of his subjects. More trustfully and deeply than any one else, Nature let him into her confidence, so various and delicate and so piercing were his perceptions. And, with all his rich command of individualities, he was a far-reaching generalizer, a sure thinker; and thus his multifarious work, both as Artist and Naturalist, has a clean fidelity as well as rare vividness.

Goethe lived in constant intimacy with Nature; he delighted to consort with her in all her moods. A year or two after his arrival in Weimar, while rebuilding his "garden-house," he slept out-of-doors wrapt in his cloak. On the 19th of May, 1777, he writes to Frau von Stein: "Last night I slept on the terrace under my blue cloak, awoke three times, at twelve, two, and four, and at each time there was a new glory around me in the sky." Here is another passage which shows the spirit in which he worked. It occurs in a note to Herder in 1784: "I hasten to tell you of the fortune that has befallen me; I have found neither gold nor silver, but that which gives me inexpressible joy, the *os intermaxillare* (intermaxillary bone) in man! I compared the skulls of men and beasts in company with Loder, came on the trace of it, and lo! there it is."

Sympathy with Nature, delight in her aspects, her phenomena, her procedure, is the most solid foundation for competence in Art. Nature ever dominates Art; as Shakespeare says,

"Nature is made better by no mean,
   But Nature makes that mean; so, o'er that art
   Which, you say, adds to nature, is an art
   That nature makes."

A chief source of Goethe's preëminence is the union in him, each in such high degree, of the poetic and the scientific, the two cardinal

tendencies of human faculty. All men have
some capacity for classification and for apprehension of law, which is the initiatory movement toward science ; and science is simply
knowledge methodized ; and all men have some
feeling for the beautiful, which is the primary
element of poetry. But to have both these
tendencies combined, each with liveliest im-
pulsion, and opportunities for their play, together with length of years, has been given
only to the preëminent German poet-sage.
Shelley is the only other great poet who, to
the love of nature native to all poets, added
a love for investigating her phenomena ; but
Shelley died before even the summer of life
had sunned his faculties into ripe productiveness. Coleridge was metaphysical rather than
scientific, and Wordsworth's intense love of
nature was sentimental, not intellectual. In
the age of Shakespeare and Milton Science
had not unfolded itself into organic form.

Goethe was a great, I had almost said a
sublime, naturalist, so high were his gifts for
enjoying, for apprehending, for interpreting
nature. He was at once a poetic and an intellectual lover of nature, — nature, that vast
mysterious presence, in which and by which

we live, whose outward aspect is for us an hourly wonder, an unfading charm, and whose inward movement is a deeper wonder, revealing forever fresh power and beauty to man, — man, a spiritual, intellectual, conscious creature, and yet a child of Nature, his being so closely interwoven with hers that he is partly her vassal, partly her lord. Of this mighty, mysterious, myriad-organed power Goethe was a favorite, but not a spoilt, child (there are no spoilt children of Nature, only of fortune), a favorite from his docility to her teachings, his disinterested love of her, his delight in her profusion, his openness to her manifold attraction, his cheerful recognition of her multiplex, kindly, inexorable law. Through his love and obedience, from vassal he came to hold much of the privilege of lord.

Goethe was too genuine a naturalist to be fond of metaphysics or of ecclesiastical theology. As a master-mind he apprehended them, and discerned their unavoidable subjectivity, and thence their one-sidedness and insufficiency. He was not, as Coleridge says of himself, "early bewildered in metaphysics and in theological controversy." In after years Coleridge deplored the having in his youth given

so much time to what in his *Biographia Literaria* he calls "this preposterous pursuit," from
which he had been, he says, happily withdrawn by awakened interest in poetry; and
he reiterates his condemnation in the following emphatic passage: "Well would it have
been for me, perhaps, had I never relapsed
into the same mental disease; if I had continued to pluck the flowers and reap the harvest from the cultivated surface, instead of
delving in the unwholesome quicksilver mines
of metaphysic lore. And if in after time I have
sought a refuge from bodily pain and misman-
aged sensibility in abstruse researches, which
exercise the strength and subtlety of the understanding without awakening the feelings of
the heart, still there was a long and blessed
interval, during which my natural faculties
were allowed to expand, and my original tendencies to develop themselves, — my fancy,
and the love of nature, and the sense of
beauty in forms and sounds."

As in Coleridge it was the poet who de-
tected the defect of abstract research, when
uncheered and unguided by the maternal
voices of nature, in Goethe it was both the
poet and the naturalist; for the sound natu-

ralist refuses to build with imaginings or assumptions, which are the chief resource of the theologian and the metaphysician. At the same time Goethe, being a large thinker, a man of ideas, with an originating mind, a mind in such close contact with nature that, as was said of Kepler, he "could think the thoughts of God," he would have curtailed his high privilege, maimed his mental action, had he refused to let his thought have its full sweep in surmising, in conceiving, in imagining the procedure of nature. The capacity to discover a law of nature involves a power of somewhat preconceiving it. Without this power — a very high, uncommon one — of originating ideas within the mind, the mind could not put itself upon the track to discover a law of nature. With profound insight Kant lays down the position: "What truth soever is necessary and of universal extent is derived to the mind by its own operation, and does not rest on observation and experience." The inductive method supposes, of course, a capacity in the mind to class and coördinate facts, and the power to coördinate facts involves necessarily the power to preconceive, before making the induction, the law that rules them.

To congenial, piercing minds nature gives hints, and such minds delight in taking such hints, in seizing at a glance, by a flashing imaginative process, a law, or the elements of a law. These rich guesses, these prolific imaginations, before they can be used as safe building material, are to be subjected to strictest tests. This union of theorizing creative meditation with scrupulous and efficient verification by induction of facts, this it is that constitutes Goethe's claim to the title of great naturalist. Reason, which is the arbiter in all investigations conducted by man, in whatever sphere,—reason is an interior, invisible might. *They who seek the reason of all things from without preclude reason*, is the import of the motto to one of Coleridge's philosophical essays in *The Friend*. Never was a man more susceptible than Goethe to impressions from without, more eager for facts; and, at the same time, never one carried within himself a stronger, clearer light to sift and class facts and to detect their governing law. The naturalist, to be great, must have, like Goethe, a philosophic mind, that is, a mind which loves to search for, and can reach, first principles.

But to this part of Goethe's greatness **must**

not be given too much of our limited time. His best moods he gave to poetry. Fresh poetry can only be written in the best moods that a man is capable of. When Goethe could write poetry, he wrote that and nothing else. When inspiration folds the faculties in its glowing embrace, they become insensible to all save its breathings. That Goethe devoted so much thought to science proves the rich fullness of his mental endowment, and that when he could not write poetry he had the spring and strength and means for centring his attention on the next highest work, — into which, too, he brought some of his creative power. He had easy command over the differing mental instrumentalities which science and poetry work with. When producing poetry he was obeying subjectively and irresistibly the most emphatic will of God as to himself; when intent on discovering the laws of nature, he was finding out objectively what is the will of God.

The creative gift constitutes the poet: to make, to create, is the meaning of the Greek word from which the term *poet* is derived. By virtue it is of his livelier sympathy with being that the poet is empowered to, humanly, create, to reproduce, being. He has a keener apprehension of, a warmer feeling for, life. Through the intensity of this feeling he can imaginatively re-live another's life, and thus represent it from within, — re-live another life, as he re-lives his own daily life through inward motion. Only what is thus brought forth, by help of light from the beautiful, is poetry, is creation. Fresh poetry must come from the inmost self, and that self must be so deep and true as to hold more humanity than one man's share, and is thus able, is impelled, to throw off fragments of humanity that shall be as veritable as those we meet on the market-place. From this teeming fullness comes the inward urgency, the spontaneous flood.

Like all the most abundant and vital and honest minds, Goethe was eminently spontaneous. He wrote, not only from within outwardly, but from an inward pressure. He did not take up promising subjects from without and adorn them ; but a feeling shaped itself within him, thus weaving for itself a fresh body, — the true creative process, whereby the generative spirit makes the material in which to embody itself. At other times he adopted a form already known, and reanimated it, re-baptized it ; thus, by means of his inward fire, putting a new soul into an old story, and by regenerative power giving fascination to an un-promising subject, causing it to sparkle with fresh movement, through the quickening life of genius, working with clean, warm human sympathies. Much verse is written in the opposite way. Acceptable, attractive subjects are deftly, gracefully treated with more or less poetic spirit. Old popular themes are taken in hand, to be reëmbodied, a new face is given to them, — but no new soul is breathed into them. Even the great friend of Goethe, Schiller, worked much in this fashion. He was ever casting about for subjects. In one of his letters to Goethe he complains of a dearth of them. Goethe never felt this dearth : in him subjects bubbled up abundantly from the spring within. He could afford to give up subjects to his friend, as he did William Tell.

To this exuberance of feeling, this readiness of sympathy, Goethe added largeness and fine-ness of intellectual faculty, which, assiduously cultivated, gave him command of strong, flex-ible, intellectual implements, so that he pos-sessed a rarely complete equipment for the high function of poet and artist, and could bring within the range of his Art an unusually full circle of human interests.

Goethe was one of the wisest of men. This implies a rich humanity of nature. To be very wise a man must enjoy that penetrating, easy vision into the most subtle, as well as the most necessary, human relations, which is only enjoyed when keenest intellectual arrows are tempered in a flood of disinterested feeling. Goethe's wisdom makes the permanent attraction of his writings, verse as well as prose ; for the best poetry, to be the best, must issue from the warm depths where tenderness is by intellect ingeniously wrought into adamantine chains of meaning.

Along the lines of Goethe's pen wisdom sparkled like verdure along the path of a spring-swollen brook. To his larger works it gives their weighty import and their inwardness of beauty, interlacing their fibre with golden threads of significancy. On distich and quatrain and other short poems wisdom glistens like solitary diamond on a white, supple finger. Take this as a sample :

> " Do thou what 's right in thy affairs :
> The rest 's done for thee unawares."

Or this :

> " Nothing could make me deeper moan,
> Than being in Paradise alone."

Or this :

> " To sweetly remember and finely to think,
> Is tasting of life at its deep inmost brink."

Or this :

> " When in thy head and heart it stirs,
> How bettered could thy doom be ?
> Who no more loves and no more errs
> Had better in his tomb be."

Or this :

> " For what is greatest no one strives,
> But each one envies others' lives :
> The worst of enviers is the elf
> Who thinks that all are like himself."

Many pages might be filled with similar brill-
iants.

Goethe said of Heine that he wants love.
From its abundance in himself he knew the
value and high import of this element in literary production. To his own pages this supreme attribute of mankind gives mellowness,
imparts to his plots and characters a higher
specific gravity. This controlling humanity
of feeling turns the Pagan Princess *Iphigenia*
into a Christian heroine ; gives arterial color

and rounded fullness to all the personages of
that beautiful idyllic epic, *Hermann and Dorothea*, — ideal personages who, through the poetic potency of their maker, seem more real
than their living counterparts in a small German town ; makes of *The God and the Bayadere* the most significant, the most profound,
and the most exquisite of ballads ; pervades
the wise pages of *Wilhelm Meister*, and is the
very soul of the mastership that presided over
the birth and growth of that marvelous creation *Mignon*.   This perfusive fellow-feeling
steeps all Goethe's writings in its life-strength-
ening current.   And this man has been called
cold !   So has been that controlled volcano,
Washington.   Goethe once said : "The most
important thing is to learn to rule one's self.
If I gave way to my impulses, I have such as
might ruin me and all about me."

The love of man was in Goethe accompanied,
I may say surmounted, by what may be termed
the uplifting, the transfiguring element in the
poetic organization, — vivid consciousness of
a transearthly spiritual world, enfolding our
earthworld, — living belief in a hereafter, where
the spirit, man, divested of his clay-clothes,
shall continue to live and to advance.   This

soaring element is as active in Dante as in
Homer, working the evolution of one of the
richest products of human genius, the *Di-
vina Commedia.* This belief inspired Milton
with our great English Epic, is an awful presence in *Hamlet,* and the animating principle
of Wordsworth's immortal ode. It hallows
the conclusion of both parts of *Faust.* At the
end of the last sublime scene of the First Part,
when Margaret, about to be executed, exclaims :

> "Thine am I, Father! save me!
> Ye Angels, ye holy ones, guard me,
> Camp ye around here to ward me.
> Henry, I shudder for thee!"

and Mephistopheles, like the consummate
worldling that he is, pronounces :

> "She is judged!"

comes a voice from above :

> "She is saved!"

The moral grandeur of this utterance is con-
current with its æsthetic beauty. The terrible
gloom needed a flash of redeeming light; the
agonizing sympathy with Margaret longed for
a solace. To draw this voice from Heaven
Goethe's tenderness of nature was backed by
his faith.

19

Towards the end of the Second Part, at the moment of the death of Faust, his soul is snatched away from Mephistopheles by Angels, one of them singing:

> "Who bestirs him, striving ever,
> Him can we surely deliver."

As they bear Faust upward, he is met by Margaret attended by bands of Angels, singing:

> "Almighty Love upbuildeth all,
> And saves them even when they fall."

Goethe sends Margaret and Faust to Heaven, because he believed in it for himself. Being a good as well as a great man, and having absolute faith in the "Almighty Love," his was not at all a religion of fear. "At the age of seventy-five" he once said to his secretary, Eckerman, "one must, of course, think frequently of death. But this thought never gives me the least uneasiness, I am so fully convinced that the soul is indestructible, and that its activity will continue through eternity. It is like the sun, which seems to our earthly eyes to set in night, but is in reality gone to diffuse its light elsewhere." And again, on another occasion: "I could in nowise dispense with the happiness of believing in our

future existence, and, indeed, could say, with
Lorenzo dei Medici, that those are dead for
this life even who have no hope for another."

Goethe's belief was not notional, it did not
come from the mere understanding partially
illuminated by the finer emotions, as does so
much of what is called religious belief ; a kind
of belief which is not truly religious is, indeed,
only formal and dogmatic, and is apt to be
accompanied by intolerance, and especially by
pharisaism. Goethe agreed with the devout
Joubert, who says : "We know God easily,
provided we do not constrain ourselves to de-
fine him." The God of sectarians is a subjective God, made after the image of the secta-
rian, in whose organization are predominant,
not the nobler disinterested emotions, but the
understanding and the self-seeking impulses.
The religious faith of an emotional man with
large reasoning range, like Goethe, is objective. Goethe believed in the immanence (to
use a technical term) of the creative spirit in
all nature ; but he, at the same time, believed
in a transcending Mind, that sustains and
rules the whole. Sensuous as was his nature,
it was so large and fully furnished that, while
never seeking to know intellectually the un-

knowable, and especially not drawing imperative dogmas out of assumptions and imaginations, he had within, in his higher consciousness, a deep, strong feeling for the invisible
spiritual, the far and yet near supernal, the
vast, celestial, inscrutable Might. And thus
in *Faust*, in the great ballads of the *Bayadere*
and the *Unfaithful Boy*, he delights to round
off with a limitless atmosphere, sending the
reader's imagination into the Infinite.

For Goethe as for Joubert it was not difficult to "know God," because their aim, and
at times their struggle, to live obediently to
his will brought them nearer to him, and their
glowing gifts clarified their vision for the divine perfections.

There is but one way to know God, and that
is to live his law. This Goethe was ever striving to do, ever aiming to better himself morally, spiritually, intellectually. Living under
the momentum of a never-remitted aspiration,
he lived the highest life that the individual
can live. And Goethe, a man of genius and
superior mental powers, having lived this high
life more busily, for a longer stretch of years
than almost any other man, his writings, in
which the best and brightest of him is skill-

fully embodied with purest art, are, to any
competent reader, a most profitable and en-
riching study. Filling more than fifty volumes, in their manifoldness and their extent
they almost form a literature of themselves.
And to these are to be added thousands of letters, happily preserved, and given to the world
in six volumes of correspondence, during ten
years, between him and Schiller; six volumes
of that with Zelter, during thirty years; three
volumes, running through half a century, of
notes and letters to the Frau von Stein ; two
volumes between him and his noble friend and
Sovereign Karl August, for fifty-two years ;
two with Knebel, covering the long space of
fifty-seven years; besides a series of single
volumes to Lavater, to Jacobi, to Merk, to the
Countess Stolberg, to Voight and others ; and
three, lately published, of letters written between his fifteenth and twenty-sixth years to
his youthful friends and companions, — the
whole forming a collection of the most valuable letters from one man ever published or
penned, the most intellectual, fluent, lively,
wise, honest, — a vast varied correspondence,
disclosing the affectionateness and dutifulness
of his nature, the breadth and depth of his
knowledge and culture.

Thus lived this illustrious man his long life, ever seeking truth ; by love of it moved to send forth his rare capacities on many paths in the search. A gentle nature, though so energetic : no bitterness in his being. Hardly was he capable of hatred : this was almost a defect in him. And his other defects? Have you nothing to say of his faults? Nothing. A man's faults — save in people of one-sided selfishness — are mostly perversions of useful qualities, perversions which, under healthiest conditions, could not be. Especially is this the case with one of so compact and complete a mental organism as Goethe. Such a man's faults are temporary misdirections of sound impulses and appetites. In a full, rounded, active nature, defects are interwoven with excellences, — are not to be divided from these without laceration ; they make part of the motion and exceptional glow of the individual being.

From those perversions which sometimes disfigure the characters even of good and great men, Goethe was singularly free. He was not vain, he was not proud, he was not envious ; he was aspiring, but not ambitious, nor avaricious, nor covetous of others' goods ;

nor was he narrow or prejudiced. He was a just man and a generous; charitable he was and genuinely religious, dutiful, forbearing, more exacting towards himself than towards others. Within his best being Goethe carried an ideal, to which he strove to conform his daily doings,— an ideal so clean and high that those who have taken on themselves to sit in adverse judgment on him could not conceive of, could hardly understand.

That the possessor of such varied, brilliant, and solid gifts strove ever, in the exercise of them, to approach a lofty standard, which only a poet who was a good man could erect and keep before him, to this it is owing that to ponder and endeavor studiously to fathom his life and life-work is an enjoyment, a discipline, a progress. He charms and instructs us, as he charmed and instructed his contemporary acquaintance. In his opening career at Weimar he so captivated all by his sympathizing ways, his playfulness, his genius, that Knebel wrote of him: "He rose like a star; every body worshiped him." And that star has had, will have, no setting. Niebuhr, the historian, well versed in the characteristics of great men, said of him: "He towers above all

whom Germany has produced." Bürger, the
poet, called him "The astonishing magician."
The greatest and the least who came into close
contact with him loved, admired, trusted him.
The brothers Humboldt, and other statesmen
and philosophers and highest teachers, all acknowledged their obligations to him. Some
of them sought his company to refresh and
strengthen their minds. The noble, enlight-
ened ducal family of Weimar, through three
generations, have continued the worship of admiring love towards the friend and benefactor
of their house. Wieland and Herder, his illustrious contemporaries and neighbors, were
comforted by his friendship, elevated by his
genius. Schiller said of him: "If he were not
as a man more admirable than any I have
ever known, I should only marvel at his genius
from the distance. But I can truly say that
in the six years I have lived with him, I have
never for one moment been deceived in his
character. He has a high truth and integrity,
and is thoroughly in earnest for the Right and
the Good."

Earnestly, indefatigably, faithfully, resplen-
dently, did John Wolfgang Goethe work
through fourscore years, cultivating his com-

prehensive, many-sided, musical mind; his soul so high-strung, that to him the singing of the spheres, the divine rhythm of creation, was more audible than to most men; and so superbly gifted that he could echo it in the choicest tones of wisdom and poetry. Born in Frankfort-on-the-Main the 28th of August, 1749, he breathed his last in Weimar on the 22d of March, 1832, tranquilly, without pain, seated in an arm-chair beside his bed. In full possession of his great faculties, he went up to higher spheres, where Dante and Shakespeare awaited him. The last words from his lips, just before he expired, were, " MORE LIGHT."